PORSCHE Boxster
The Complete Story

Other titles in the Crowood AutoClassic Series

AC Cobra	Brian Laban
Alfa Romeo Spider	John Tipler
Alfa Romeo Sports Coupés	Graham Robson
Aston Martin DB4, DB5 and DB6	Jonathan Wood
Audi quattro	Laurence Meredith
Audi TT	James Ruppert
Austin-Healey 100 & 3000 Series	Graham Robson
BMW 3 Series	James Taylor
BMW 5 Series	James Taylor
BMW M-Series	Alan Henry
BMW: The Classic Cars of the 1960s and 70s	Laurence Meredith
BMW Z Series	Mick Walker
Bubblecars and Microcars	Malcolm Bobbitt
Citroën DS	Jon Pressnell
Datsun Z Series	David G Styles
Ferrari Dino	Anthony Curtis
Ford RS Escorts	Graham Robson
Imp	George Mowat-Brown
Jaguar E-Type	Jonathan Wood
Jaguar Mk 1 and 2	James Taylor
Jaguar XJ Series	Graham Robson
Jaguar XJ-S	Graham Robson
Jaguar XK Series	Jeremy Boyce
Jensen Interceptor	John Tipler
Jowett Javelin and Jupiter	Edmund Nankivell and Geoff McAuley
Lamborghini Countach	Peter Dron
Lancia integrale	Peter Collins
Lancia Sporting Coupés	Brian Long
Land Rover – Series One to Freelander	Graham Robson
Lotus and Caterham Seven: Racers for the Road	John Tipler
Lotus Elise	John Tipler
Lotus Esprit	Jeremy Walton
Mercedes-Benz Saloons: The Classic Models of the 1960s and 1970s	Laurence Meredith
Mercedes SL Series	Andrew Noakes
MGA	David G Styles
MGB	Brian Laban
MG T-Series	Graham Robson
Mini	James Ruppert
Morgan Three-wheeler	Peter Miller
Porsche 911	David Vivian
Porsche 924, 928, 944 and 968	David Vivian
Range Rover – The First Generation	James Taylor and Nick Dimbleby
Range Rover – The Second Generation	James Taylor
Rolls-Royce Silver Cloud	Graham Robson
Rolls-Royce Silver Shadow	Graham Robson
Rover P5 & P5B	James Taylor
Rover SD1	Karen Pender
Saab 99 and 900	Lance Cole
Sprites and Midgets	Anders Clausager
Sunbeam Alpine and Tiger	Graham Robson
Triumph 2000 and 2.5PI	Graham Robson
Triumph Spitfire & GT6	James Taylor
Triumph TRs	Graham Robson
TVR	John Tipler
VW Beetle	Robert Davies
Volvo 1800	David G Styles

PORSCHE Boxster
The Complete Story

Gavin Farmer

THE CROWOOD PRESS

First published in 2004 by
The Crowood Press Ltd
Ramsbury, Marlborough
Wiltshire SN8 2HR

www.crowood.com

© Gavin Farmer 2004

All rights reserved. No part of this publication may be reproduced or transmitted in any form or by any means, electronic or mechanical, including photocopy, recording, or any information storage and retrieval system, without permission in writing from the publishers.

British Library Cataloguing-in-Publication Data
A catalogue record for this book is available from the British Library.

ISBN 1 86126 675 8

Designed an typeset by Focus Publishing, 11a St Botolph's Road, Sevenoaks, Kent TN13 3AJ

Printed and bound in Great Britain by CPI Bath

Contents

	Introduction and Acknowledgements	7
1	Continuing the Tradition	8
2	Gathering Thoughts	21
3	Bringing on the Style	32
4	Engines for the Future	47
5	Hidden Pleasures	58
6	Looking at the Market	70
7	Boxster Meets the Press	91
8	Improving Upon Perfection	99
9	Born for the USA	123
10	And Now for Something a Little Different, a Little Faster	130
11	New Production Technology	147
12	Owning a Boxster Today	158
13	Old Versus New: The 914 vs 986	166
	Appendix I: VIN Coding for Boxsters	174
	Appendix II: Model Year Differences	175
	Appendix III: Suspension Setting for Track Days	178
	Appendix IV: Customizing Your Boxster	179
	Appendix V: Production	181
	Appendix VI: Comparison Charts	182
	Bibliography	189
	Index	190

Introduction and Ackowledgements

By the early 1990s the famous German sports car manufacturer Porsche AG was in serious trouble. Sales were down dramatically despite the constant respecification of the admittedly long-in-the-tooth 968 – it dated back to 1976 in reality – and the evergreen 911.

Change arrived in the person of Wendelin Wiedeking, the youngest man to be appointed to the key role of Chief Executive Officer since Ferry Porsche himself. Under Wiedeking's astute leadership the plans for the company-saving 986 and 996 models were conceived and brought to market. As we now know, the Boxster has become a market success even though it was possibly viewed by some members of the Porsche AG board as somewhat radical and therefore in danger of failing. However, being a genuine Porsche has meant that its success was virtually guaranteed from the beginning.

This book is about that car, the rich heritage it carries and the people who made it all happen.

Acknowledgements

This book would never have been possible had it not been for the tremendous assistance received from the people at Porsche AG in Stuttgart. In particular, Michael Schimpke, Klaus Steckkoenig and Ulrike Keller from Porsche's Public Relations Department; CEO Wendelin Wiedeking, chief stylist Harm Lagaay; Ing Ulrich Schempp; and from the company's Historisches Archiv section, Klaus Parr, Dieter Gross and Jens Torner.

My grateful thanks are also due to Karen Angus, Andrew Davis, Ellie Gray and Steve Walker at Porsche GB; Bob Carlson, General Manager Public Relations, Porsche Cars North America; and Steve McHale from JZ Machtech in Kings Langley, Hertfordshire.

Invaluable assistance was given by Chris Horton, editor of 911 & Porsche World magazine; Nic Doczi, Matthew Bennett and Claire Eason from the Porsche Club Great Britain; and Stephen Mummery, editor of the Porsche Post club magazine

Further thanks to Ken Kinnersley from the MR2 Owners' Club for information on the MR2; Erica Haddon from Toyota for photographs; Peter Newton from Fiat and Alfa Romeo; Samuel Holl from Mazda; David Ingram from Audi; Linda Robinson from Nissan; James Griffiths from Honda; Rob Halloway from DaimlerChrysler; Chris Willows from BMW; Kevin Jones from MG-Rover and Roger Parker from the MG Owners' Club, all of whom provided information and photographs.

And finally, my thanks to the following for their assistance in providing information and photographs: Natalie Campana from RUF Automobile GmbH in Pfaffenhausen; Susan Childress from Roock North America in Roswell, near Atlanta, Georgia; Uwe Gemballa at Gemballa Automobiltechnik GmbH & Co KG in Leonberg; Ralf Niese at TechArt Automobildesign GmbH in Leonberg; Marita Niemann and Nico from Strosek Auto Design GmbH in Utting/Ammersee; and Ferdinand Pietz from Turbo Tuning Pietz in Kolbermoor.

Photographs are courtesy of Porsche AG unless otherwise noted.

Gavin Farmer
Surrey

1 Continuing the Tradition

Early Years

Dr Ferdinand Porsche really started something when he conceived the Auto Union Type A racing car first seen back in 1933. Apart from the Mercedes *Tropfenwagen* racing car from the early 1920s, all racing cars and practically all production cars had their engine up front driving the rear wheels – the classic *système Panhard*.

By the time Porsche had created the Auto Union P-Wagen he was already something of an industry celebrity and a rebel within the conservative and very serious ranks of German business executives. From his first efforts with the electric hub-driven Lohner, he had shown a remarkable ability to think 'outside the square'. He was only thirty-one years of age when the Austrian branch of the Daimler Motor Company hired him as its Technical Director.

In the 1920s Porsche moved to Daimler in Cannstatt where he created the very fast, very powerful and very expensive supercharged Mercedes-Benz SS and SSK that helped to establish the racing career of the great Rudolf Carraciola.

During the 1920s two seemingly unconnected events took place that involved a then unknown Adolph Hitler. In 1925 Hitler was introduced by his chauffeur Julius Streck to racing driver Hans Stuck when the pair visited Stuck at his farm to do some hunting. And a year later, Hitler met Porsche at a race meeting. An unsuccessful, or turbulent depending on your interpretation, move to Steyr in Austria ended when Porsche stormed out, having disagreed with the Board on several technical matters. Fed up with being subordinate to people whom he considered to be lacking in vision, in 1931 Ferdinand Porsche established his own consultancy business – Dr Ing h c Porsche GmbH in Stuttgart-Zuffenhausen.

Ferdinand (father, left) and his protégé son Ferry, right.

Continuing the Tradition

In 1931 Stuck again met Hitler and lamented the fact that he no longer had a works drive with Mercedes-Benz or Austro-Daimler. Hitler reassured him that when he gained power in Germany he would personally make sure that Hans Stuck had a German racing car to drive. Hitler went on to assume absolute power in Germany and was named Chancellor in January 1933. At the Berlin Motor Show a month later he announced a prize of RM 500,000 to the manufacturer who could design, build and win glory for Germany on the racetracks of Europe.

The people at Daimler-Benz believed the money was theirs until a combination of events brought a second player into the arena – the newly formed Auto Union GmbH. Hitler remembered his meetings with Hans Stuck and contacted him after the motor show to ask him to make a 'wish list' for his racing car. Stuck contacted Ferdinand Porsche and the two began a collaboration that led to them having a meeting with Hitler, during which Porsche convinced Hitler that he had a racing car design ready (his so-called 'P-Wagen') to meet the new formula, and that the subsidy should be split between his company and Daimler-Benz.

Dr Ferdinand Porsche had not long established his bureau in Stuttgart as a consulting engineer to the automobile industry (and anybody else who was willing to pay his fees) and had definite ideas about car design. His first contract was with Wanderer, a member of the Auto Union combine. It was not difficult for the persuasive Porsche to convince the Board of Directors at Auto Union to consider favourably his new racing car, and for it to be

Father and son discussing details of the Type 60 project, the Volkswagen Beetle.

Continuing the Tradition

A favourite of Hitler and Porsche was the wealthy and socially well-connected Hans Stuck who helped develop the specifications for 'his' German racing car.

A pensive Ferdinand Porsche studies his most radical creation, the mid-engined Auto Union V16 racing car. Only a few brave drivers could extract the speed potential from these brutal machines.

manufactured in the Horch plant in Zwickau, because the engineers and craftsmen employed there understood the fine tolerances necessary for success in the top level of racing.

The impact of the Auto Union Type A must have been considerable when it was given its first public outing back in 1934. The appearance of the car was completely different from everything that had gone before, and the placement of the engine behind the driver was viewed with a high degree of scepticism. There it was on the racetrack, sleek in its silver livery with the stub exhausts from its V16 engine poking skywards – the bellow from them must have been both ear shattering and unbelievable!

Stuck now had his German racing car, and he was to prove over the next five years to be one of the few men who was capable of taming the power and handling characteristics of the various Auto Union racing and record cars. Only the brave and charismatic Bernd Rosemeyer and the diminutive Italian Tazio Nuvolari together with Stuck were able to get the best out of these tremendously powerful and fast machines.

Unfortunately, most of the Auto Union racing cars were found by the Russians in the aftermath of World War II and were stacked on rail cars and carted back to Moscow, where they were callously disassembled or broken up because the Russians understand neither the

The most spectacular and successful driver of Porsche's Auto Union V16 racer was ex-motorcycle champion Bernd Rosemeyer. A most charismatic man, he would die at the wheel of the streamliner while attempting a speed record on the Frankfurt–Darmstadt autobahn.

technology involved nor the (capitalist) value of what they had confiscated. Thankfully, several enthusiastic Westerners smuggled enough parts out during the Cold War era to build two cars; more have been recovered since the Velvet Revolution and Audi AG has spent millions recreating the Type D and Bernd Rosemeyer's record car.

After hostilities were over, Dr Porsche's family moved the business to Gmünd in the Austrian Tyrol, where plans were drawn up for a sports car that would be based on Volkswagen running gear and carry the Porsche name. Actually, two mid-engined cars were conceived at that time – the famous Cisitilia Grand Prix car, the Type 360, that had a supercharged 1.5-litre horizontally opposed twelve-cylinder 'boxer' engine with a four-wheel drive transmission system; and an actual Porsche sports car. The Cisitilia was designed and built for Piero Dusio to race, the money paid to Porsche GmbH being used to gain the release of Ferdinand Porsche from the French authorities, who had imprisoned him in 1945 for his alleged collaboration with the Nazis.

On 8 June 1948 the first fruit of those sports car efforts was born – the Porsche Type 356. Its Erwin Kommenda-designed body was both minimalist and sleek, with the suggestion of an aerodynamic form. There was space for two people in the cockpit and situated immediately behind them – in the mid-engine position – was a Porsche-modified (the cylinder heads had angled exhaust valves and a slightly higher compression ratio) 1,131cc edition of the Porsche-designed flat-four air-cooled 'boxer' engine sourced from the emerging Volkswagenwerke in Wolfsburg, far to the north in Germany. Power output was a meagre 40bhp at 4,000rpm, but it was enough to push the aerodynamic roadster to a maximum speed of 84mph (135km/h).

The first sports car to carry the family name, the 356-1 at Gmund with its creators.

The lone Porsche 356 with its tiny 1,100cc engine competing at LeMans, 1951, where it finished twentieth overall and first in class.

Only a handful of the Porsche 356s were made with this configuration before Ferry Porsche – the son of Ferdinand Porsche and now managing the business – decided to reverse the position of the engine and the gearbox, and install them in the same way that Volkswagen did in its ubiquitous Beetle. For the remaining years of Porsche 356 production the definitive formula had been established – rear-mounted air-cooled boxer engine driving the rear wheels through a four-speed transaxle.

In fact, that formula has become *de rigueur* at Porsche ever since.

Racing Success

Racing the product was never very far from the thoughts of the Porsche people, and so it surprised no one when a Porsche was entered at the 24 Hours of Le Mans in 1951. It was a

Continuing the Tradition

The Porsche 550 Spyder displayed at the Frankfurt IAA in 1955, with the company's famous PR manager Huschke von Hanstein at the far left.

tiny aluminium-bodied coupé powered by an 1,100cc boxer engine. Amazingly, it finished twentieth overall and won its class, the drivers being Auguste Veuillet and Edmond Mouche.

That success put Porsche on the international stage, with inquiries from the lucrative American market following. Max Hoffman and John Neumann were two key people who guided Porsche's success in that country, Neumann being a successful racing car driver in his own right.

Various Porsche racing cars over the decades have been successful with the mid-engine configuration, the first of these being the famous Type 550 Spyder, with its complex but powerful Type 547 Ernst Fuhrmann-designed quad-cam 1.5-litre boxer engine that produced an amazing (for the time) 110bhp at 7,800rpm. First shown to the world at the Paris Motor Show on 1 October 1953, the 550 has been variously described as not only mid-engined, but also a sports car of alluring beauty. For Porsche, it was a critically important car because it was very successful on the racetracks of the world, proving to be virtually unbeatable in the 1.5-litre class. In 1954, for example, it won its class in the Mille Miglia, the 24 Hours of Le Mans, the 12 Hours of Reims and

Legendary racing driver Hans Hermann at the wheel of a 550 Spyder in the 1951 Carrera Panamerica race. Success in these races was the source of the name Carrera used on many future Porsches.

Continuing the Tradition

the infamous Carrera Panamerica. For film buffs, it was a Spyder that screen idol James Dean was driving when he was killed.

A mere seventy-eight Porsche 550 Spyders were produced – they cost a staggering DM 24,600 in 1954, with the equally immortal Mercedes-Benz 300SL costing DM 29,000. The impact of the Spyder was far greater than the numbers produced would suggest.

The Spyder led to the development of the famous Porsche 718 RSK, a startlingly focused lightweight racer. Some people might call the RSK 'minimalist', as it was pared down to the most basic of essentials required to carry out its role successfully in the company's plans. Its 1.6-litre version of the Fuhrmann engine produced 140bhp at 7,500rpm and could power the car to speeds of 160mph (257km/h)! An RSK driven by Barth and Seidel was victorious on the Targa Florio circuit in Sicily in 1959 and again in 1960, when it was driven by Swede Joachim Bonnier teamed with the Formula 1 driver Graham Hill.

Following the RSK in 1960 was the RS60, a development that did the David and Goliath act at the 12 Hours of Sebring in 1960, when it won outright against a field of Ferraris, Maseratis and other far more powerful cars.

For 1961 Porsche developed the RS61, followed by the 718 W-RS that was powered by a 210bhp (at 8,200rpm) air-cooled flat-eight of 2-litre capacity. Development continued and by 1963 the W-RS was available in either Spyder or coupé form with fibre-glass body panels and, another Porsche first, a coil-and-wishbone suspension system. Bonnier again won the Targa Florio in 1963, this time driving a 718 W-RS coupé, while Edgar Barth was crowned European Mountain Champion in a 718 W-RS in 1964.

Porsche also flirted with Formula 1 in the early 1960s; apart from Dan Gurney's win in the French Grand Prix at Rouen in 1962, this was not a time of joy for the company. Sports cars were the company's speciality and so they

Count von Trips driving a 718 RSK in the Gaisburg hill-climb event in 1958. The power–weight ratio for the RSK was enormous –142PS, 530kg! Von Trips drove many Porsche sports racing cars with success.

Continuing the Tradition

retired from GP racing to concentrate their resources on that category.

In the mid-1960s, Porsche introduced the limited-production 904 with its Ferdinand Alexander 'Butzi' Porsche-designed body made from fibre-glass, a first for the company. It was at once both svelte and aerodynamic, to the point of creating an impression of speed even when standing still. Under the fibre-glass body was a steel backbone chassis carrying a fully independent suspension system and a powerful (180bhp at 7,200rpm) 2-litre quad-cam four-cylinder boxer engine located immediately behind the two-seater cabin. The 904 would prove to be a most versatile racer, winning on race circuits, hill-climbs and in rallying – the Monte Carlo with Eugene Böhringer driving, for example. The 904, and its big brother the 906 that was powered by a 210bhp 3-litre flat six-cylinder engine, has gone down in Porsche folklore as one of the more outstanding designs to emanate from this most fertile of companies.

American racing driver Dan Gurney in the 1962 German GP in the Typ 804 F1 car. It was not a successful season for Porsche.

The 550 Spyder evolved through the 1950s with steady development; this is the Typ 718 RS60, 1960.

One of the most beautiful Porsches ever built was the 904, here in prototype form, 1963.

Below *The Hollywood actor and sometime racing driver Steve McQueen at speed in the Typ 908, 1970.*

Above *The 904 began a sports-racing revolution at Porsche. The 907, here at the Nürburgring in 1968, was a part of that growing family of super-successful sports-racing cars.*

Continuing the Tradition

A famous photograph showing the twenty-five examples of the 917 long tail lined up for inspection for homologation purposes.

The 906 had a brilliant, but short, career – just the one year, 1966 – but this programme led inexorably to the most exciting period of sports car racing ever known to enthusiasts all over the world, and in particular Porsche enthusiasts. From the 906 Porsche developed the 907 and 910 that were powered by 2-litre flat-six and 2.2-litre flat-eight engines (the latter developing up to 270bhp and giving the car a maximum speed of around 190(!)mph (306km/h)). This in turn led to the 908, with its powerful (but still air-cooled) 3.0-litre eight-cylinder 350bhp (at 8,500rpm) boxer engine, followed by the fabulous 917 of 1969.

With the 917, Porsche dominated the world sports car competition, winning Le Mans in 1970 and capturing the international sports car title in both 1970 and 1971. Then rule changes in Europe led Porsche to cross the Atlantic and challenge the so far all-conquering McLarens in the Can-Am series in North America. The European 917 was powered by an air-cooled flat-twelve engine of 4.5-litres and had a body that was supposedly optimized in the company's wind tunnel. However, the combination of 585bhp, lightning-quick acceleration (0–100mph in less than 4sec!) and high-speed instability tested even the bravest of Porsche's pilots. The taciturn Englishman, John Wyer, formerly with Ford, stepped in and solved the aerodynamic instability with the simplest of solutions – cutting off the long tail and putting a fixed spoiler on the rear.

For the Can-Am series Porsche developed a larger flat-twelve engine, one of 5.4-litres and initially 650bhp, but it was not nearly quick enough to stay with the 8-litre Chevrolet-engined McLarens. So Porsche turbocharged the engine (as you would!) and for the amazing 917/30 1,100bhp (and up to 1,500bhp in qualifying) was extracted from the flat *zwölfzylinder* boxer engine in which the late Mark Donohue in his bright blue-and-yellow liveried Sunoco-Porsche+Audi absolutely

Continuing the Tradition

Two Porsche 917s in Gulf-Wyer livery at the famous Spa circuit, 1971.

trounced the opposition in 1973 Can-Am season.

Porsche continued with race car developments after the 917 with cars such as the 936 and 956, but the most successful ever Porsche racer was to come – the 962. It won more races over a longer period of time that any Porsche race car before or since. And the common thread here? The mid-positioning of the engine, of course!

Arrival of the 914

Collaboration with the Volkswagenwerke brought the then largely unloved (but now far more valued) 914 on to the market in late 1969 after it had been displaying at the Frankfurt IAA that year. It was a Porsche designed and engineered sports car powered at first by the anaemic VW 1.7-litre boxer four-cylinder engine (taken from the equally unloved VW 411 saloon) that produced just 80bhp at 5,000rpm with a Bosch fuel-injection system. As an expensive option buyers could specify the more powerful 2.0-litre flat six-cylinder engine from the 911. Its styling was controversial at the time and is probably still regarded as somewhat controversial today. That aside, it was practical in a way that only the NSU Wankel-Spider was insofar as it had two luggage compartments – one at the front and one at the rear, where the detachable Targa roof could be stowed. Its road dynamics were pure Porsche, but people seemed unable to accept its rather Germanic appearance.

Gradually, Porsche developed the design, as the company always does. In 1973 a more powerful 1.8-litre fuel-injected boxer four-cylinder became available, and the following year the 914 came to be powered by a fuel-injected 2.0-litre flat-four engine from the heavily revised VW 412. The Porsche 911 engine option had been discontinued in the 914 very early in its career. Surprisingly, the final iteration with the VW 2.0-litre engine was almost as fast as the original Porsche ex-911-powered 2.0-litre version and, although

Continuing the Tradition

The VW-Porsche 914, here in basic 1.7-litre guise, was a result of a VW and Porsche collaboration. Despite ungainly looks, it was a commercial success.

Below Left *Porsche entered a 914-6 GT in the gruelling 84 Hour Marathon de la Route on the famous old Nurburgring circuit. The 914-6 was reliable, handled superbly and was quick, but not quick enough to win.*

Below *As with the Marathon, the 914-6 ran like clockwork but was not quick enough for victory.*

no longer selling in the numbers VW wanted, it was badged as a Porsche (the VW badges disappeared in 1972), with sales trickling on until the 924 superseded it. Today there is an awakening to the virtues of the 914 as these cars are appreciated for their technical ingenuity at a time when sports car design was in the doldrums.

The Porsche 914 did enjoy its proverbial fifteen minutes of fame; actually it was twenty-four hours. A 914 was entered for the 1970 24 Hours of Le Mans, driven by two Frenchmen, Guy Chasseuil and Claude Ballot-Léna. It ran faultlessly for the race, finishing sixth overall and first in the GT Class.

Despite all predictions, the evergreen 911 was still the company's mainstay in the market, even though the marketing people at Stuttgart-Zuffenhausen had tried to kill it off by surrounding it, first, with the budget-priced (for a Porsche) 924 and its derivatives, and then the expensive V8-engined 928. Water-cooled front-mounted engines driving the rear wheels through rear-mounted transaxles powered both the 924 and 928. Both underwent the normal 'evolution' process for which the company is so famous and both sports coupés were made more desirable over the years.

But in the hearts and minds of the Porsche diehards, they were not real Porsches.

Left and Below
Porsche's magnificent response to the Ferrari Enzo and other super cars: the Carrera GT. It's more like an über-Boxster!

Moving On

Porsche's clientele expected their cars to follow the tradition that was the company's signature, a tradition that had been developed by the 356 and followed by the 911, that of rear engines of the boxer configuration with air-cooling. New emission laws governing exhaust gases and noise levels were, however, becoming more and more difficult to pass with an air-cooled engine, which meant that new avenues had to be explored.

The fact that Porsche has returned to produce a mid-engined sports car that has been positioned below the fabled 911 in the company's range should have come as no real surprise. What possibly is surprising is how long it has taken for the Boxster to appear.

And to show the confidence of the now extremely successful and profitable company, Porsche has released the fabulous Carrera GT to top its burgeoning range. Like the Boxster, the Carrera GT is mid-engined, powered by a mighty 5.7-litre water-cooled V10 engine that produces an enormous 612bhp and 425lb ft of torque which can propel it to speeds in excess of 200mph (322km/h). Look closely at its styling and you can see Boxster influences in many, many aspects.

2 Gathering Thoughts

Porsche management was caught between a rock and a hard place. As the decade of the 1980s progressed into the 1990s the company's position in the marketplace deteriorated dramatically. The traditionalists within the company were pushing to keep the 911 in production and were urging the development of a 'junior 911'.

However, the stronger faction at the time was pressing ahead with new developments of both the 924 and 928 to make them even more desirable. For them, the future was irrevocably linked to water-cooled front-engined sports coupés. They had even authorized the designing and building of a one-off Porsche 989, a four-door sedan that looked just superb, but in the words of chief stylist Harm Lagaay, 'It was not the right type of car for Porsche at that time even though its styling was a success.'

The 924

The 924 that was introduced to the world in 1976 (the styling of which is credited to Harm Lagaay, interestingly enough) was not a 'true' Porsche by Porschephile definition because it was powered by a water-cooled in-line four-cylinder. Not realized by many was the fact that Audi's then head of Research and Development, Ferdinand Piëch, was keen for the

Porsche's famous research and engineering centre where the Boxster (and many other Porsches) have been created.

Gathering Thoughts

EA425 car to be powered by one of his forthcoming in-line *fünf-zylinder* engines, but its length mitigated against this in a compact sports coupé. The power unit selected for Projekt EA425 was an unrefined 2-litre cast-iron unit bought in from Audi. Its roots went back to the high compression (11.5:1 in 1964!) 1.7-litre ohv unit designed by Ludwig Kraus for the Audi Super 90 of 1965. The Super 90 was a member of the new family of cars developed out of the F102, the last of the two-stroke cars built by the post-war Auto Union. Further development saw this engine's compression ratio progressively lowered and its capacity expanded to 1,871cc, still with ohv, for powering the new Audi 100 sedan released in 1968 and the Audi 100 S coupé in 1969; and then finally to 1,984cc (86.5 × 84.4mm bore and stroke) and with a single toothed belt-driven overhead camshaft operating bucket-type tappets with tapered screw adjusters. For installation in EA425 it had to be tilted 40° to the right to squeeze under the very low bonnet line. In addition, a finned alloy sump was made for its application in the EA425 and a forged crankshaft replaced the original cast-iron shaft.

The whole 924 project – this number being nothing more than a marketing name and not a Porsche type number – was another collaboration with VW (EA425) that dated from 1972 when a formal agreement was signed between Porsche and Volkswagen for a sports car to replace the relatively successful 914. It came about when Rudolf Leiding replaced Kurt Lotz as head of the huge Volkswagenwerke AG in 1971 and immediately cancelled Projekt EA 266, the underfloor-engined prototype that Porsche was developing to replace the immortal VW Beetle. To appease his detractors, he instigated the EA425 project as a successor to the 914.

In 1974, with the world recovering from an

The humble 1.9-litre ohv engine from the Audi 100 S coupé formed the basis of the 2.0-litre sohc engine of the original 924. (Photograph courtesy of Audi GB)

Early days – little did anyone realize that the basic shape of the 924 (here in original 1976 form) would remain for nearly two decades. Note the clean and simple lines.

oil crisis and VW having its share of difficulty in reinventing itself – the company was on the brink of bankruptcy – as it slowly broke free from the yoke of the Beetle, VW exited the development programme when it decided that the sports car market was not where it wanted to be. VW allowed Porsche to purchase the project for DM 100 million and to badge it as one of its own, and build it in the ex-NSU works in Neckarsulm. It was the right move for Porsche at the time but nobody was fooled, however.

It is true that early examples of the 924 were basic in ways that were most un-Porsche like. Power from the Bosch K-Jetronic fuel-injected engine was a paltry 125bhp – US versions had a meagre 95bhp at first! In typical Porsche fashion, there was an immediate programme of extensive development to improve the 924 and to save face in the midst of a media storm about the car. Interior appointments were high on the agenda, as was increasing the engine's power output and performance.

In August 1978 production began of the 924 Turbo. With its 170bhp turbo engine it reached a maximum speed of 140mph (225km/h) and ran the 0–100km/h (62mph) sprint in 7.8sec according to factory sources. A minor revamp for the 1981 model year saw the power raised to 177bhp. Small production runs were made of the 924 Carrera GT with its intercooled turbo engine that produced 210bhp, the GTS with a 245bhp engine and finally the racing GTR with 375bhp, which the factory said would run to 181mph (290km/h) and 4.7sec for the 0–100km/h sprint.

To make the 924 more acceptable and appealing to sports car buyers who would pay the Porsche price premium, the company had to equip it with a 'proper' Porsche engine. Buyers had to wait until late 1981 (model year

Gathering Thoughts

To bolster the image and performance of the 924, Porsche introduced the extremely quick 924 Turbo, complete with optional two-tone paint scheme and multi-spoke alloy road wheels.

1982), with the release of the 944 powered by a completely new sohc in-line four-cylinder engine of 2.5-litre capacity. It was a parallel development to the V8 engine designed for the 928 and was an all-alloy unit with two balancer shafts for improved refinement. Digital Motor Electronics (DME in Porsche-speak) in conjunction with Bosch L-Jetronic fuel injection saw output at 163bhp at 5,800rpm. This was not a huge increase over the final versions of the 924 (almost as much as the 924 Turbo), but torque was a solid 151lb ft at 3,000rpm.

The 944

Development continued with a completely restyled dashboard appearing for the 1985 model year, and at the same time the company announced the 944 Turbo with an eight-valve cylinder head, a KKK *turbolade*r and 220bhp. A further capacity increase took place for the 1987 model year when it was raised from 2.5 litres to 2.7 litres, still with the eight-valve cylinder head. Power rose slightly to 165bhp and torque to 166lb ft at 4,200rpm. Performance was now far more acceptable, maximum speed off the showroom floor rising from 131mph (211km/h) to 137mph

Development and evolution continued to improve the 924, here with 928-style alloys.

One of the nicest Porsches ever built: the 944 Turbo Cabriolet. It had storming performance, style and character.

(220km/h), acceleration from 0–100km/h dropping from 8.4sec to 8.2sec. At the end of the 944 era, which was from 1986 through 1992, further engine upgrading saw the capacity increased to a full 3 litres for 1989 (944 S2), with a new double ohc sixteen-valve cylinder head that allowed the one engine specification to meet all international emission requirements. Power rose to 211bhp for the 3-litre engine.

The final iteration of this design appeared in late 1991 for the 1992 model year – the 968. It was the best of the line but was greeted with muted enthusiasm by the world's media, who viewed it as old (not entirely incorrect) and somewhat stodgy in styling (also not entirely incorrect). The 968 was essentially a 944 with a nose and tail restyle, plus the addition of the Porsche-patented VarioCam mechanism on the camshaft drive to vary valve timing and improve the responsiveness of the engine. Power output rose to 240bhp at 6,200rpm and torque to 225lb ft at 4,100rpm. The 968 engine was a four-cylinder development of the V8 that powered the 928 S4, the two engines sharing many components.

To spice up the range, Porsche introduced the 968 Club Sport, which retained the 240bhp engine, and the Turbo S edition, in which the engine was rated at 305bhp at 5,400 and a monstrous 369lb ft at 3,000rpm. The final 968 was built in July 1995, many months before the Boxster would appear.

The Controversial 928

Developed virtually in parallel with the 924 was one of the most controversial production Porsches ever – the 928. It was designed and indeed intended to replace the 911 eventually

Gathering Thoughts

The S2 had the full 3-litre dohc engine for 140mph performance and superb dynamics.

according to company representatives, but of course it never did. Both the 928 and 924 shared a similar architecture: front-mounted water-cooled engine driving the rear wheels through a rear-mounted manual or automatic transaxle joined rigidly to the engine by a tubular shaft through which passed the drive shaft.

The Porsche 928 debuted at the 1977 Geneva Motor Show where it created quite a sensation, and was crowned later that year as the 1978 European Car of the Year. It was controversial in ways the 924 never was or could be, mostly due to the exalted status accorded to it by Porsche at its release. It was an extremely logical design (to Porsche), conceived and produced by eminently logical and highly intelligent Porsche engineers. It's just that the traditional Porsche clients did not see it that way!

The company's view was that the 911 had a limited life and as the 928 had been designed with all future safety and emission requirements allowed for in the design it would take the company into new market areas and attract former Mercedes-Benz and Jaguar buyers, with maybe some BMW, Ferrari and Aston Martin clients being drawn into the web.

The 928 was virtually the opposite of the 911 in every way: water-cooled V8 versus air-cooled flat six; front-engine versus rear-engine; traditional styling versus very non-trad styling; excessive avoirdupois (in the opinion of many) versus comparative light weight. The only common denominator was power, and lots of it. It was, in fact, that rather rare beast in today's automotive world, a 'clean sheet' design

Gathering Thoughts

Nearly the end of the line that began in 1976. By now the 968 looked old and the interior was cramped, but it still offered unrivalled performance and handling.

Even with the aero additions for the CS version, Porsche could not hide the age of the coupé. That did not hamper the driving experience, however.

in much the same way that the Boxster would be some years into the future.

A relatively slow-revving V8 engine was chosen (against a high-revving V6), mainly because the engineers felt it would be more suitable for the critically important North American market. The first series 928s had a 4.5-litre sohc per cylinder bank all-alloy engine that developed 240bhp at 5,500rpm and 257lb ft of torque at 3,600rpm, which pushed the 3,750lb (1,700kg) coupé to 60mph from rest in 8.0sec and ran a 138mph (222km/h) top speed. Not lost on the Porsche cognoscenti was the fact that the bigger, heavier and more expensive 928 was, for all of Porsche's hyperbole, slower than the 911!

Engineering sophistication was everywhere, most famously in the patented rear suspension, the so-called 'Weissach Axle', in which the bushes were designed to prevent the rear wheels from toeing out when accelerating, braking or cornering. Developments of this technology would appear later in the Boxster and 911.

By 1980 the 928S had appeared with a 4.7-litre V8 and 300bhp at 5,500rpm and 283lb ft

A most underrated and unappreciated Porsche, the 928 was the ultimate autobahn stormer when released and only got better with age and development.

of torque at 4,500. Acceleration was now 6.2sec for the 0–60mph sprint and top speed rose to 155mph (250km/h). Now only the 911 Turbo was quicker.

Big improvements were made to the 928 series that appeared at Geneva in 1987, the S4, with a full 5-litre capacity and new cylinder heads featuring dohc per head and four valves per cylinder. These cylinder heads were shared with the four-cylinder engine in the late 944 and 968 cars. The S4 boasted 320bhp at 6,000rpm and 317lb ft at 3,000 for a top speed of 168mph (270km/h) and 5.9sec for the 0–100km/h sprint. The 928S4 was now significantly faster than the 5.3-litre V12 powered Jaguar XJS and much closer to Ferrari.

By September 1988 there was the 928 GT with 330bhp and in 1992 came the last, and best, of the 928 series: the 928 GTS. This coupé had the 5.4-litre V8 with dohc per cylinder head and a massive 350bhp at 5,700rpm and 362lb ft at 4,250rpm on tap for a 0–100km/h time of 5.7sec and a maximum speed of 171mph (275km/h).

Technically sound, and beautifully designed and made though the 928 was (the 924 was less of each attribute), neither model was a true Porsche in the sense that they did not appeal to Porsche's traditional buyers. The 924/928 families of coupés actually brought many thousands of new clients to the fold; very few existing clients were swayed by the sales arguments for either of them, however. No, they continued to buy the faithful and ever-evolving air-cooled 911 in sufficient numbers to keep it in production.

Gathering Thoughts

The S4 came with the 320ps 5.0 V8 and would run to 168mph (270km/h) given the opportunity. It was a superb touring machine.

Into the 1990s

At the beginning of the 1990s Porsche was in financial trouble, with its very existence under threat. As CEO Wendelin Wiedeking said:

> Our manufacturing costs were too high, production was not efficient enough and the development of new products took too long. Moreover, model policy had partially failed. When, on top of this, the exchange rate for the US dollar plunged it suddenly became very clear that Porsche was no longer competitive. There was a massive slump in demand for our sports cars in the most important export markets – above all North America – and Porsche was in the red.

Sales had plummeted, as had earnings, to the point where industry experts were predicting either the demise of the famous family-owned company, or at the very least its absorption into a much larger combine like Volkswagenwerke AG.

Porsche entered the 1990s with a three-model range: the 944 (soon to become the 968); the evergreen 911; and the 928. From the outside it appeared as if the company wanted to abandon its heritage – rear-engined sports coupés that exuded character – in favour of the new generation with their water-cooled engines up front and their transaxles out back. Thoughts about another line of production sports cars were frequently discussed, but resources were stretched to the limit as the company emerged from an economic trough during which the whole management structure was reorganized.

Porsche kept tinkering with the 928 and with the GT version offered 330 ps and 170mph (275 km/h) performance.

Wendelin Wiedeking

Wendelin Wiedeking is an interesting man, a driven man in some respects. Born on 28 August 1952 in Ahlen, Westphalia, Germany, he attended the Aachen Technical University from the age of twenty and graduated at the age of twenty-six as a Diplom-Ingenieur.

He then worked and studied as a member of the scientific staff at the laboratory for machine tools and industrial management at the Aachen Technical University, where he gained his doctorate from the mechanical faculty in December 1983.

Wiedeking's first job was with Porsche AG, interestingly enough. He was employed as the assistant to the director of production and materials management, where he gained a valuable insight into the workings at Porsche AG that would stand him in good stead some years later.

In 1988 he was lured away from Porsche and Stuttgart by Glyco Metall-Werkekg, Wiesbaden, where he was appointed as manager of the technical department. His skills and expertise were quickly recognized and within two years he was appointed managing director at Glyco.

In 1991 he was back at Porsche as the director of production and material management, the same department in which he had previously worked at the company. Clearly Porsche had noticed his talent because the following year he was appointed spokesman for the Board and in 1993 he was became President and Chief Executive Officer of the company.

Since then he has restructured the company, instigated a completely new production system and fostered a new model strategy that has been spectacularly successful. He has been the recipient of many industry awards.

Central to the successful revival of Porsche was Wendelin Wiedeking, today Chairman of the Board. Following his appointment, change began almost immediately. In late 1991 the situation had been desperate, but by early 1992 a two-model plan was decided upon and agreed within the company. The recently released 993 version of the 911 – the last of the 'traditional' air-cooled 911s – would be replaced by a completely new Projekt 996, and a smaller, less expensive model coded Projekt 986 would be developed concurrently and, for economic reasons, would share many components. Simultaneous engineering was the phrase coined by Porsche at the time. It was planned that the two new models would be developed and in production for the 1996 model year.

Market research carried out at this time showed the emergence of a subtle but nonetheless significant shift in the buying patterns of people, a pattern that would favour Porsche if it could design, develop and manufacture a new model in time. It was, in many ways, a time of transition away from the traditional family sedan and station wagon and the crudely engineered off-road four-wheel drives to a far more sophisticated market in which so-called niche models would dramatically increase in sales volume. The research pointed to a dramatic growth in sales of off-roader vehicles, convertibles and roadsters, and talked of a growing number of affluent childless couples who were more critical in their assessment of their motoring needs.

Porsche reasoned that its planned 986 would add further momentum to this trend and fulfil the demands of its target group in terms of individual style, non-conformity and sportiness. And, through its brand name, it would express high status on the social scale.

The new 986 sports car would be positioned and priced well below the existing (and forthcoming) 911 and would be responsible for attracting a new clientele to Porsche, buyers who would not be impressed by high prices but by value for money. Studies carried out by Porsche indicated that buyers of the Boxster would be people pursuing young, trend-oriented and sporting leisure-time activities like mountain bike riding, windsurfing and snowboarding. By comparison, the 911-buyer profile showed them to be more interested in tennis, squash and skiing. Indeed, the 986 was designed to attract to Porsche a far younger buyer profile – an average age of thirty-five years compared with forty-four years for 911 buyers.

Another group of people important to Porsche were the so-called 'empty nesters', well-off but active senior citizens. Further research showed that many people who had bought a roadster earlier in the 1990s, when Mazda in particular had rekindled enthusiasm for the genré, would regard a Boxster as the next step upwards in their ownership experience. This same research also indicated that owners of coupés derived from mass-production sedans, and therefore anything but exclusive, would also see a Boxster as offering them a higher social status.

Porsche's Director for Research and Development, Wolfgang Durheimer has responsibility for the successor to the Boxster.

3 Bringing on the Style

The Boxster Concept

If any particular event or moment in time was the spark for the Boxster, it was most likely the Tokyo Motor Show held during October 1991. Porsche's chief designer, Harm Lagaay was there with Grant Larson and his reaction was quite straightforward:

> Audi displayed their AVUS show car that looked gorgeous and there were several other concept cars on show from Japanese and European manufacturers, all of which excited me. I faxed back to my studio and began collecting ideas in the form of sketches from designers back home. I said to the Board of Directors (all of whom were with me in Tokyo) 'We need to do a show car.' The directors agreed with me, as they felt, as I did, that it would bolster confidence in the Porsche name and demonstrate the innovative spirit within Porsche.

Early in 1992 a new model strategy was developed and approved by the Board. From there, the ball started rolling. As anybody who has the slightest interest in Porsches already knows, the inspiration for the Boxster's styling was rooted in the company's long and illustrious sporting heritage – to be specific, the famous 550 Spyder and RSK racers.

The Audi concept car that sparked Harm Lagaay's imagination for Porsche to design a concept car. (Photograph courtesy of Audi AG)

Bringing on the Style

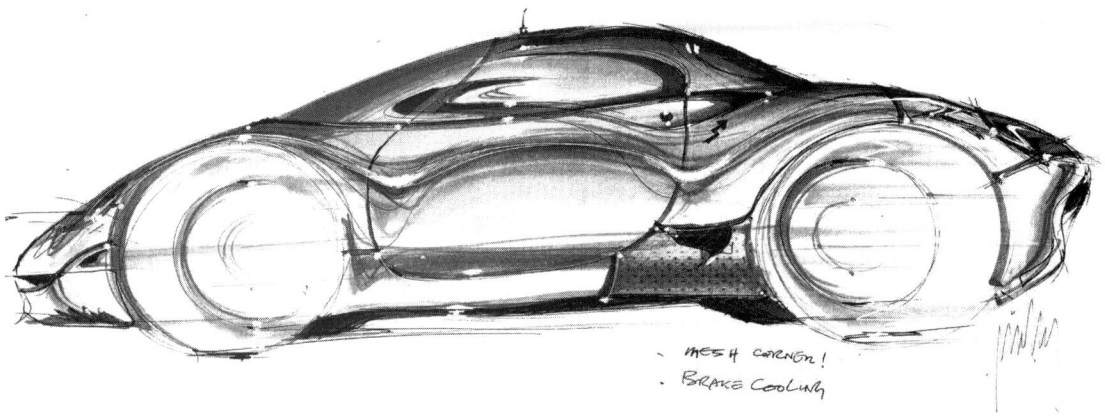

An early sketch, probably drawn by stylist Pinky Lai, exploring possible styling themes.

During the autumn of 1991, immediately following the Tokyo Show, Grant Larson began developing the concept car in one studio at Weissach. Its construction began in the spring of 1992, the aim being to display it at the forthcoming Detroit motor show in January (winter) 1993.

As Lagaay said when interviewed by John Lamm for his book Porsche Boxster: 'Grant is a very important designer in the history of the concept car because he handed down many of the essential design elements. And he put everything the show car had on the production version.' He added: 'I had an interior designer called Stefan Stark. The chief modeller who did most of the work and was able

---

Grant Larson

Grant Larson played a critical role in the development of the Boxster's design. Born in Billings, Montana, on 9 May 1957, he began his journey to international fame at the world-renowned Art Centre College of Design in Pasadena, California, from which he graduated with Distinction having completed a Bachelor of Science degree in Transportation Design. He continued his studies at the Milwaukee Institute of Art and Design in Milwaukee, Wisconsin, from which he graduated with a Bachelor of Fine Arts Degree in Industrial Design.

After an apprenticeship Brooks Stevens Design in Mequon followed by several steps up the career ladder, Larson spent the 1980s working in the General Motors Advanced Aero Studios, where he sketched proposals for future vehicles and also spent time working on the (sadly aborted) mid-engined Corvettes. This was followed by three years as a freelancer with the Design Club in Japan before venturing to Germany and Audi in Ingolstadt, where he worked as an exterior designer in the Advanced Design Studio. Projects worked on here included proposals for the third generation Golf and Polo as well as the Audi A4.

It was only a short drive along the autobahn west to Stuttgart when the call came to work for Porsche AG. Larson was employed as an exterior designer and was part of the team that created the aborted 989 and the current generation 911; he created the 1993 Boxster show car and was chiefly responsible for the 1996 production version of the Boxster as well as the Carrera GT show car that was shown at the Paris Auto Salon in 2000. The follow up to the 996 released in 2004 was also Larson's responsibility.

Today he is the manager of Advanced Design – Exterior and is charged with fostering that inimitable Porsche style successfully into the future.

Bringing on the Style

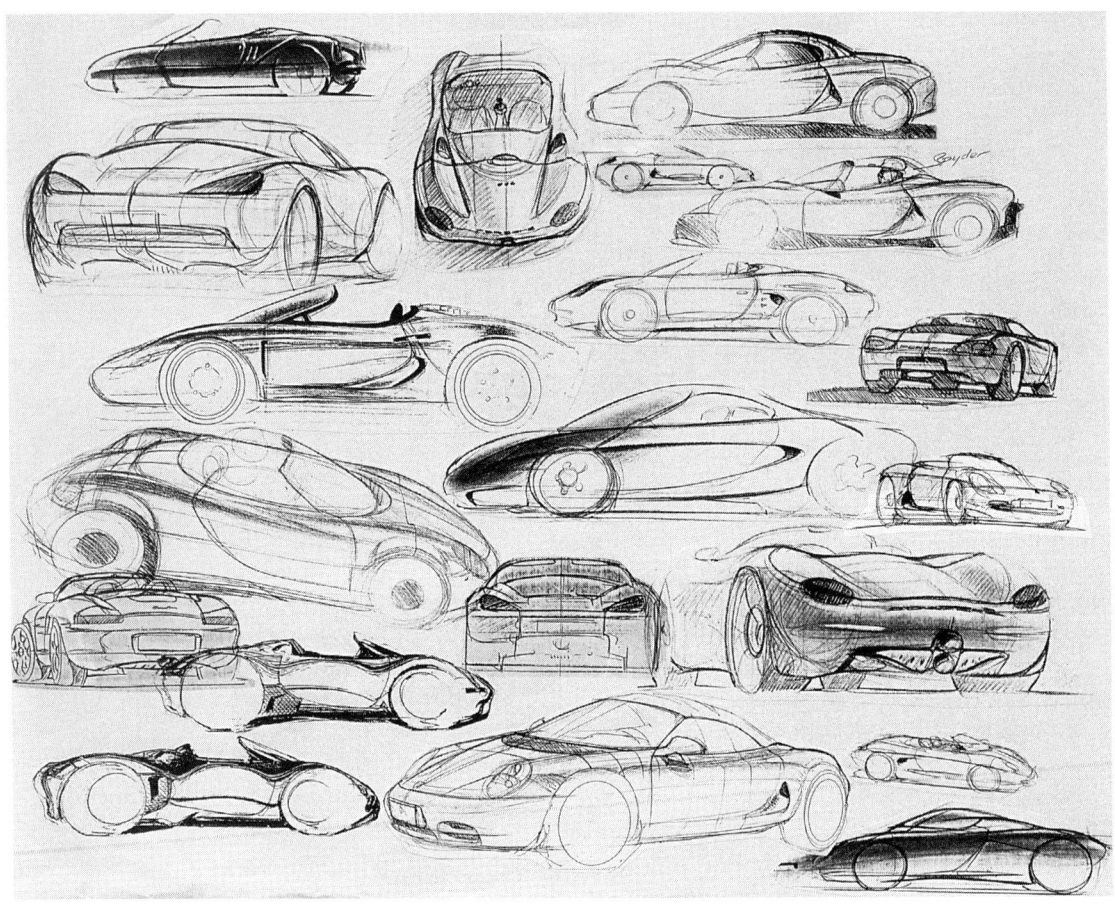

A beautiful montage of sketches from Porsche Design showing the diversity of ideas expressed by the team as the Boxster's styling evolved towards the concept car.

to interpret everything we were sketching and talking about was Peter Müller. Those were the three guys who did the shape of the show car.'

The question soon arose: What should we call the concept car? A competition took place within the Design Studio and the Press Department. After several hundred possibilities had been reviewed, Lagaay favoured the name 'Boxster' that was proposed by Steve Murkett. The name was derived from the word boxer, the flat engine configuration, and roadster.

According to Lagaay: 'It had a punchy, more emotional kick to it, rather than just a few numbers. We felt that this new car from Porsche deserved more than just a number designation, but a real name.'

It seems hard to believe today, but the shape and proportions of the show car took some time to evolve. Early editions appeared to both Lagaay and Larson to be too high, or the rear was too short, the wheelbase was too long, and so on; all part of the normal refining process of any car design. Larson and Müller, in particular, persevered and kept on refining the design until they were satisfied that its proportions were absolutely right.

During this time – mid-to-late 1992 – the design team began to realize that, as good as

A Grant Larson sketch that is remarkably close to the production Boxster.

the show car was, it was going to be far too small for the production version. Lagaay again:

> We didn't change the show car; we went on with that, but we did change the package for the production car. We were not satisfied with the proportions that were developing out of the production car package, and therefore had this little study going on in another studio. The show car helped us define our goals and provide a vision.

There were a number of interesting features on the concept car that obviously pleased Lagaay and his design team. The interior air vents had tiny fans in them to increase the flow of air through them; the car had a traditional Porsche five-pod instrument arrangement with back-lit dials that was jointly developed with VDO; there was a see-through 'bridge' over the dials; a digital display screen in each instrument; his 'n' hers seats; a motor woofer; and the 'pea-shooter' centre exhaust. Neither the seats nor the woofer saw production, although several of the others did, albeit in slightly modified form.

According to Lagaay, 'Porsche has a rich history of mid-engined cars. The very first Porsche and the 550 Spyder in 1954 and the

Larson supervising rear styling details.

Construction of the concept model continues.

Making the interior; note the rear suspension and disc brake and the five-dial instrument cluster.

Further exploration of the concept, this time as a hardtop coupé.

later 718 series race cars. For the Boxster the message was clear: use these as inspiration, their proportions, and their charisma. Typical Porsche elements should be reinterpreted in a new way without appearing retro:

> We saw the Boxster as a reinterpretation of Porsche mid-engined themes, most importantly the prominent fender treatment, the 'valleys' and low bonnet that they form inside the fenders. This could be seen as a sort of minimalisation of masses. This feeling from the past was also reinterpreted in the interior. Body colour was brought inside to give the impression of a car designed as a complete unit.

There were two facets to the 986 programme: to design a concept mid-engined show car;

Bringing on the Style

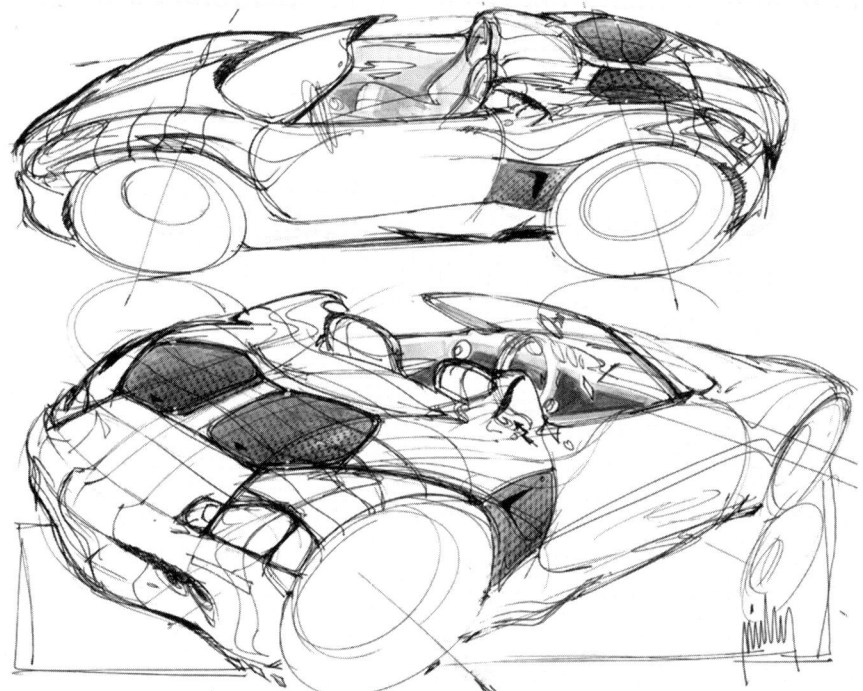

More sketches from Pinky Lai.

and to design a production mid-engined roadster. Both programmes were run in parallel. In addition, the Projekt 986 was that relatively rare event in the automobile industry today – a 'clean sheet' design where it would be all-new from front to rear, with no components carried over from a previous model. Such opportunities come along all too infrequently and so designers must grab the occasion with both hands and do something special, something memorable.

Meanwhile, the production design was being developed in an adjoining studio by a group of four designers – Wolfgang Moebius, Matthias Kulla, Pinky Lai and Steve Murkett. Interestingly, the styling ideas that each had

---

Harm Lagaay

Harm Lagaay is by far the most 'international' of the senior people in the Boxster story. He was born in Den Haag, Holland, on 28 December 1946 at a time when the country was rebuilding from the rubble of war. His parents migrated to British Borneo (today Brunei), returning to Holland in 1960.

After studying at the Institut for Automobiltechnik (I.V.A.) in Driebergen, Lagaay took his first job at the publishing company Olyslager in Soest, Holland, where he was a technical illustrator. He moved to Simca, then quite a big player in the European market, where he had responsibility for their technical documentation. His first break into the world of automobile design came when Porsche hired him in 1970. He stayed until 1977, having worked on various styling upgrades to the evergreen 911, various racing cars and the 924.

This was followed by an eight-year stint as the Design Manager in the Advanced Studios of Ford AG in Cologne. A four-year spell was enjoyed with BMW Technik GmbH in Munich, where he was the Chief Designer and was responsible for the BMW Z1, a car of unusual construction (various plastics of varying thicknesses, steel backbone chassis and drop-down doors) and today very collectible. In January 1989 he moved back to Porsche, where he was appointed Chief Designer. Lagaay retired at the end of 2004.

Bringing on the Style

A Grant Larson sketch of the concept car.

sketched independently of the others were remarkably close in broad concept. The team, all bearing in mind the Porsche spirit, look and feel, drew hundreds of sketches. They concentrated on defining the most important elements that made up a Porsche in their view: the dominant cylindrical fenders; low flat bonnet; round or oval headlamps; V-shaped shut lines; narrow waist in plan view with muscular fenders; a strong shoulder running fore-and-aft from the doors to the fenders and the characteristic descending back end.

A package was laid out in which the basic physical dimensions were established, for example the wheelbase, windscreen position, driver's position, overhangs, wheel tracks and so forth. Lagaay and his design team had to 'play around' with the proportions when it became obvious that the front and rear overhangs were going to be longer than anticipated.

Regarding the 'face' of the Boxster, Lagaay said:

> The look of a car is often judged by the face it expresses. We did not want to wander away from our history of oval headlamps, but decided to reinterpret them. We came up with the idea of an all-in-one headlamp, which includes all five functions, and wrap it in a free-form package blending it nicely with the Boxster's forms and tying in into the shut lines. These describe the form of the body and the lamp elements.

The development of the production design had been under way for about a year, but progress was being hampered by the lack of proportions in the model. The problem, or

Rear three-quarter view of the Larson 1:1 clay model of the production version of the Boxster. Apart from details like the side air vents and rear bumper shape, this is the Boxster.

challenge, was created by the need to house the two engine cooling radiators behind the front bumper. However, their size 'bulked-up' the front of the car and destroyed its beautiful proportions. In the autumn of 1993 the critical decision was taken to enlarge the whole car.

The Finer Details

Developing the styling theme was only one aspect of the 986 project. Equally as important was the issue of packaging, the complex task of positioning each and every component in the automobile. Within the given dimensions of the future Boxster the team had to find room for two people (whose heights could likely vary from around 5ft tall to 6ft 5in). In addition, they had to fit the engine in the limited space behind the cockpit, find room for the radiators for the engine's cooling system, and

Key People Involved in Creating the Boxster

Show Car

Harm Lagaay, Chief Designer
Grant Larson, Exterior Designer
Stefan Stark, Interior Designer
Otto Geffert, Studio Engineer
Peter Müller, Lead Modeller

Production Car

Grant Larson, currently Manager Advanced Design Exterior
Stefan Stark, currently an independent designer, also for Porsche
Matthias Kuffa, currently Manager of the 911 model range
Steve Murkett, currently Manager of the Cayenne range
Pinky Lai, currently Manager of the Boxster model range

Bringing on the Style

The Pinky Lai 1:1 clay model; it is much higher at the rear (for aerodynamic reasons) than the final version.

luggage space that could accommodate at least one set of golf clubs.

It was also important at this stage to consider such seemingly mundane items as doors that opened wide enough for easy entry and exit, and a soft-top that would be easy to operate (it had been decided that it would be electrically operated, not manually), and would fit snugly and stow neatly. The optional hardtop would need to be easy to install and be totally weatherproof.

Hand-in-hand with the development of the Boxster's exterior styling was the crucial issue of aerodynamics. According to Lagaay:

> Having a good Cd figure was important, but equally we were seeking excellent coefficients of lift. By smoothing out the underbody we were able to lower the Cd by around 6 per cent, but, more importantly from a high speed stability point of view, we were able to reduce the lift at the front of the body by an amazing 36 per cent!

A 1:1 clay model showing two themes, the left side by Wolfgang Moebius, the right by Grant Larson. Note the lack of side air vents and the rear deck height.

The aerodynamicists at Porsche have never been afraid of a challenge, having learned many valuable lessons in automobile aerodynamics with the 911, a car that many experts and critics consider to be extremely difficult to 'tame' because it is rear-engined and therefore has a rearward weight bias, with a sloping rear design that mitigates against simple aerodynamic solutions. In many ways, the air-cooled

Bringing on the Style

A 1:1 clay model from Pinky Lai. Note the very 993-like front, somewhat awkward side air vent shape and virtually straight door shutlines.

A 1:1 clay model from Wolfgang Moebius, again with a very trad Porsche front, exaggerated side indicator lenses and no cooling vents.

911 helped to break down the barriers of conventional thinking regarding a car's aerodynamics – it was the world's first production car to be fitted with the movable rear spoiler that was a huge step forward for the industry.

This apparently simple device removed at one stroke of the styling crayon the necessity for a car to be fitted with a huge, ugly vision-blocking rear spoiler as witnessed by Porsche's own 'whale-tailed' 911 Turbos of the 1970s and 80s.

Stefan Stark's interior for the Detroit show car was a progressive design without being too 'way out' or impractical as many concept cars tend to be. It retained a certain 'Porscheness', if you like, and is a modern rendition of the classic Porsche style that clearly linked it to other models in the com-

41

Bringing on the Style

Larson's side of the clay model also with the high rear deck to accommodate the bulky folding soft-top. The development of the Z frame allowed the deck height to be lowered.

The front of Larson's proposal, still minus the side air vents; note the high windscreen from the 911 (996) that was later lowered.

pany's history, but added a satellite navigation system screen and four circular air vents, each with their own ventilation fan. Neat if a tad impractical!

Where the show car's dash had a five-circular instrument display, like the 911, the production Boxster's instrument pod contained only three dials, like the famous RSK that inspired it, with each of the gauges slightly overlapping each other. In true Porsche tradition, the tachometer took centre stage of the three dials and was the largest in diameter. Flanking it to the left was the speedometer, while on the right was the combination dial containing the engine coolant temperature and fuel level instruments. Cars equipped with the Tiptronic automatic had an indicator as to what range the driver was operating at the moment.

Larson's winning proposal – all the production elements are here, although they were later refined.

Additional information for the driver was provided in small semi-circular sections in the lower part of each main dial. In the speedometer are distance odometers – trip and total – in digital form, a similar digitized read-out for the car's speed and a distance-to-empty pictogram in the tachometer, while a pictogram showing the level of the engine's dry sump system occupies the combination dial along with other useful information.

The tachometer was red-lined at 6,700rpm and graduated to 7,800rpm, while the speedometer was graduated from 0km/h to 300km/h with every 50km/h being numbered – every 25mph in the UK. This is insufficient from a legal point of view in many export markets, which is why Porsche fitted the digital read-out to display actual road speed.

Lined up below the main instruments were various warning lights covering such functions as traction control, hazard warning, spoiler active, worn brake pads, low brake fluid level, low engine oil pressure, light bulb failure and so on. Porsche likes its drivers to be kept informed about their car's condition.

An intriguing aspect of the design of the Boxster's instruments was the creation of a new-look instrument needle. This may not seem significant at first until you understand that these were the first all-new Porsche instrument needles in twenty-two years!

The centre console included an integrated heating/ventilation/air-conditioning system (HVAC) with the main components coming from the Audi A4, not that you would necessarily recognize them in their new home. The graphics have been altered, but the hardware is nonetheless Audi-sourced. In the lower part of the console was the audio system with in-built provision for a CD player. Provision was also made for the installation of an optional satellite navigation system.

Apart from the increase in physical size, there were few changes that had to be made to the concept car during its transition to the

Boxster 2.5 Specifications

Engine:
Horizontally opposed six-cylinder ('boxer' configuration) with aluminium alloy crankcase and interchangeable cylinder heads, dual overhead camshafts per cylinder bank, four valves per cylinder, dry sump lubrication system, Bosch Motronic 5.2 sequential electronic fuel-injection system.

Bore:	85.5mm (3.37in)
Stroke:	72.0mm (2.83in)
Capacity:	2,480cc (151cu in)
Power:	204bhp @ 6,000rpm (150 kW)
Torque:	181lb ft @ 4,500rpm
Specific output:	82bhp per litre
Compression:	11.0:1

Transmission:
Five-speed manual or Tiptronic automatic.

Ratios:	Manual	Automatic
1st	3.500	3.670
2nd	2.120	2.000
3rd	1.430	1.410
4th	1.030	1.000
5th	0.790	0.740
Rev		
Final drive	3.889	4.205

Suspension:
Front: MacPherson struts, coil springs, tubular dampers, lower A-arms, stabilizer bar.
Rear: MacPherson struts, coil springs, tubular dampers, lower lateral links, single lower trailing link, stabilizer bar.

Brakes:
Hydraulic, twin-circuits with front-rear split, Bosch ABS.
Front: 11.7in (292mm) ventilated disc rotors, four-pot calipers.
Rear: 11.5in (290mm) ventilated disc rotors incorporating 6.5in (164mm) diameter brake drum for the parking brake.
Total swept area: 484sq in.

Steering:
Hydraulic variable power-assisted rack and pinion, overall ratio 16.9:1, lock-to-lock 3.0 turns.

Wheels:
Standard: Cast aluminium alloy, 6.0J × 16 at the front, 7.0J × 16 at the rear; tyres 205/55 ZR-16 front, 225/50 ZR-16 rear.
Optional: 7.0J × 17 with 205/50 ZR-17 tyres front, 8.5J × 17 with 255/40 ZR-17 tyres rear.

Bringing on the Style

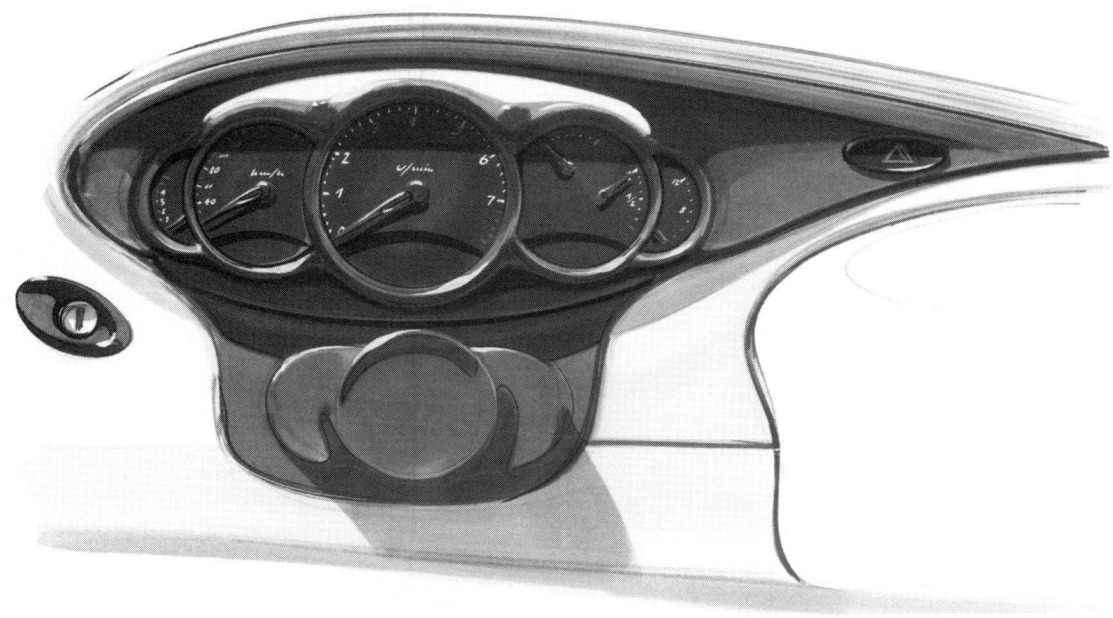

The concept car's five-dial instrument cluster.

	Boxster 2.5 Specifications *continued*			
Dimensions:				
	Length:	4,315mm (171.0in)		
	Width:	1,780mm (70.1in)		
	Height:	1,290mm (50.8in)		
	Wheelbase:	2,415mm (95.2in)		
	Track front:	1,455mm (57.3in) standard wheels/tyres		
	Track rear:	1,508mm (59.4in) standard wheels/tyres		
	Track front:	1,465mm (57.7in) optional 17in rims		
	Track rear:	1,524mm (60.2in) optional 17in rims		
	Fuel tank:	57 litres (12.5 Imp/15.1 US gal)		
	Kerb weight:	1,292kg (2,756lb)		
	Distribution:	47:53		
	Drag Cd:	0.31		
Performance:				
	Top speed	149mph (240km/h) manual		
		146mph (235km/h) Tiptronic S		
	Acceleration:	0–100km/h	Manual	6.9sec
			Tiptronic S	7.6sec

Bringing on the Style

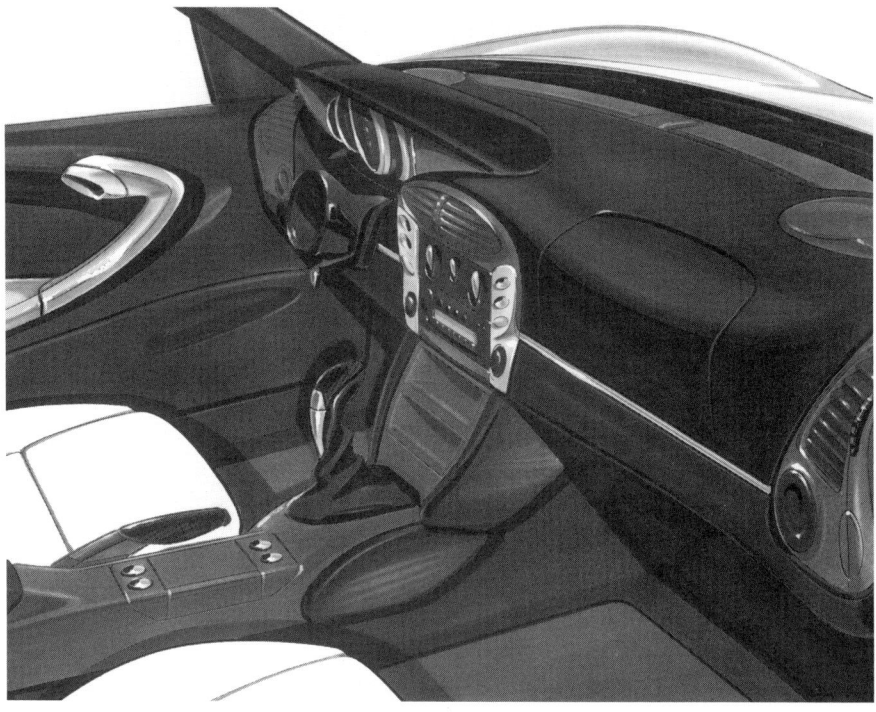

Sketch of the proposed interior layout, probably by Stefan Stark. The theme has been established here; only details would change before final production.

production Boxster. There was, of course, the necessity to commonize the frontal structure with the 996, but the benefit here was that it improved the car's crashworthiness and provided better luggage space; the side air vents had to be raised as the originals would have picked up far too much road debris; a roll bar was added; the tail light design was changed to give it a timelessness that was important; the graphics were changed as it was felt the show car's would 'age' quickly; and the area behind the cockpit was changed to accommodate the Z-folding roof.

In Stark's original interior proposal there were 'his 'n' hers' seats, but, while a neat idea, it was considered impractical and so the Boxster's seats became variations of those used in the 911.

In keeping with Porsche's environmental sensitivities, much of the interior of the production Boxster is made of thermoplastic polyolefin (TPO), which is a specially developed polypropylene material. This material has two big pluses: it does not emit any chemical odour and deposit that annoying film on the inside of the windows; and it is fully recyclable.

That the design of the Boxster has been a success is now part of automotive history. It is at once functional, elegant, purposeful and shows emotion; its philosophy retains its youthfulness as it is driven by impulses of the tradition as well as the vision of the future. Lagaay expressed it this way:

> Because a designer is always looking for ways to change and improve, the design is always in movement. This movement is persistent and passionate.
>
> Our form philosophy encompasses flowing sensual forms, yet muscular, generating a fascinating interplay of light and reflection. At the same time it is important for the customer to follow these changes. A new model should never forget its heritage and should remain flexible.

4 Engines for the Future

Höhe Technik

German automobiles have always been renowned for their *höhe technik*, their advanced technical design and specification. Where previously English, American and Japanese cars could be generally gathered under the broad heading of refined orthodoxy – that is, fairly basic overhead valve engines, basic suspension design usually with a semi-elliptic live axle at the rear and generally poor braking along with mediocre ride and handling – German cars generally espouse a higher level of technical thought.

It really does not matter whether we're talking about Mercedes-Benz, BMW, Borgward, Audi or Porsche, they all have at their core an advanced technical design for their times. Cynics would say that they are unnecessarily complicated, and by inference expensive to design, manufacture and (importantly) maintain, but that is in many ways hiding from the facts.

From the very beginning Porsches were examples to the world of extracting the proverbial quart from the pint pot. On the racetracks of Europe they became giant killers, especially in long distance endurance events where their light weight, agile handling, powerful brakes, aerodynamics and high power-to-weight ratios stood them in good stead against far more powerful opposition.

The very first Porsche sports cars featured fully independent suspension by torsion bars, aerodynamic body form, lightweight aluminium body construction over a robust steel platform and an engine and gearbox built using beautifully made light magnesium alloy castings. The production Porsches used derivatives of the Volkswagen overhead valve flat four-cylinder ('boxer') engine, while, for the most part, the competition engines featured overhead camshafts. They were complex, as the cynics and critics said, but they were powerful and effective.

Progress toward overhead camshafts for the production Porsches was signalled by the release at the 1963 Frankfurt Motor Show of the seminal 911. Not only did its flat six-cylinder engine continue the air-cooled tradition,

The first Porsche engines were mildly modified VW Beetle 1.2 litre boxer engines that produced a mere 40bhp.

Engines for the Future

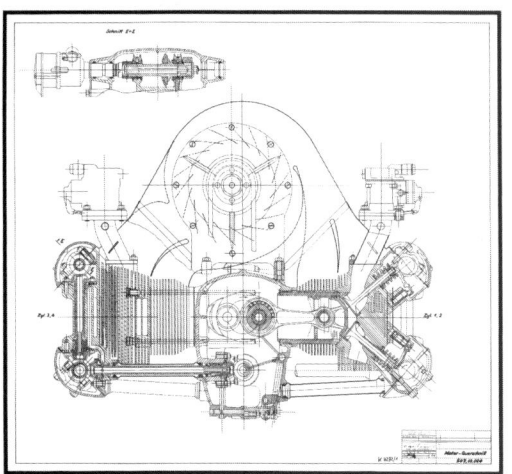

Ing (later Dr) Ernst Fuhrmann was challenged by Ferry Porsche to develop a racing engine that produced 70bhp per litre. The result was the extraordinarily complex (for the time) Typ 547 engine of 1.5 litres that produced 110bhp at 7,800rpm.

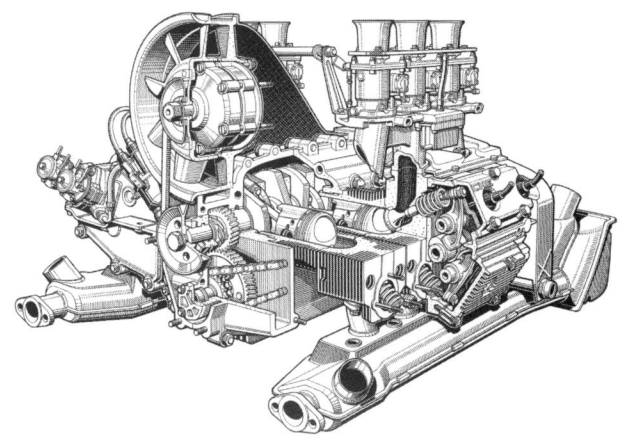

Regarded by many as the greatest Porsche engine of all time, the air-cooled flat six began life as a 2-litre and retired more than thirty years later at 3.6 litres.

but it also had a chain-driven overhead camshaft for each cylinder bank. New styling brought the coupé right up-to-date (little did Porsche or enthusiasts realize that the 'Butzi' Porsche styling would live for more than thirty years) and a redevelopment of the torsion bar independent suspension system, itself another Porsche tradition, added to the driving excitement.

As ever, more power was developed from ever-increasingly larger capacity versions of the famous flat six, with the added performance being counterbalanced by more sophisticated suspension developments that enhanced the ride and handling. Not only that, the 911 had to be upgraded regularly as new international safety and emission laws were enacted, all of which added to the cost.

With the 993 signed off for production, the designers and engineers at Porsche began considering the technical design of the 986 and 996 duo. From the lessons learned with the 928 in particular, replacing the 911 with a sports coupé with anything but a flat six-cylinder engine mounted in the rear was dicing with corporate death. A newly designed flat-six engine that would be water-cooled would power the 996, that much was certain, and with the 986 being developed in parallel, it, too, would be powered by a water-cooled flat-six engine.

Because of the close ties with Audi, Porsche did look at powering the 986 with its version of the well-proved Audi 2.8-litre V6 engine but according to Ing Ulrich Schempp, 'It was discussed briefly but the decision was made to power the Boxster with a genuine Porsche-designed (and manufactured) engine of traditional layout.'

Discussions were also held regarding powering the 986 with a flat four-cylinder engine for a so-called 'economy' version. According to Schempp:

> In the very early concept phase a four-cylinder version of the Boxster engine was also assessed.

Engines for the Future

After the 924, the 928 was the first Porsche production car with a Porsche-designed water-cooled engine. Many of the technology lessons learned on the 928 V8 were applied to the 986/996 engine programme.

The bore and stroke would have been taken over from the 996, giving a capacity of 2.3-litres. In continued examination of the aspects of technology (power, acoustics, vibrations), costs and marketing the decision was made in September 1992 to go with a 2.5-litre flat six-cylinder engine. The four-cylinder, therefore, remained a hypothesis.

When the air-cooled 911 engine was conceived maximum power and torque were the development engineer's main targets; today their task is complicated by the need to meet ever more stringent emission requirements, fuel economy and noise pollution issues.

Commenting to author Clauspeter Becker in the book *Boxster S*, Dipl.-Ing Rainer Srock said, 'In spite of all our respect for the existing engine, we could see the need for a new one that would uphold Porsche's authority in the engine design area for another lengthy period.'

Colleague Johann Georg Ulrich, who was responsible for the engine development programme, also said, 'Our task was not only to

Ing Ulrich Schempp

Ing Ulrich Schempp was born on 15 September 1946 and at the age of twenty-four, having graduated from university with a mechanical engineering degree, he joined Porsche in 1970. During his first fifteen years at Porsche he worked in the electronics division, where he was intimately involved in the development of the VW-Porsche 914, 916, 924 and 944, as well as being a key member of the team that developed the Digital Motronic unit in collaboration with Bosch. That was introduced on the 944 and 911 Carrera.

In 1985 he was reassigned within the company and appointed project manager for the 928. He was responsible for the 928 facelift and the development of the 928 GT. During this time he also had responsibility as project manager for the stillborn 989, the 986 Boxster and Boxster S, and since 1999 has had responsibility for the whole Boxster production series.

Engines for the Future

design a far better engine, but to make it at only a fraction of the cost of the previous one!'

And Ing Ulrich Schempp also noted, 'Our aim with the new family of engines was lightweight construction. We wanted a full aluminium engine encompassing new technologies in bore materials, forged crankshaft and connecting rods and hollow camshafts.'

Despite the need for change, there were certain characteristics that would be carried through from the air-cooled flat six. They were: the 'boxer' configuration of the cylinders, because such a layout meant that the engine's centre of gravity would be lower and that it could be positioned much lower in the car's body; the bore centres of the cylinders were the same 118mm, which meant that much of the existing machinery used for machining and honing could be used, thus reducing the investment need for new machine tools; and the tradition of the short stroke engine with the seven-bearing crankshaft. Everything else was new.

Not surprisingly, the major engine castings – the two-cylinder block halves and the two interchangeable cylinder heads – were cast from lightweight aluminium alloy. Unlike some rival manufacturers, and also unlike the solution chosen more than a decade earlier for the cylinder block on the 928, the 986 engine (and the 996, too) used cylinder liners that are made by the Lokasil process. This applied the required silicon only where it is needed, hence the name: Localized Silicon or Lokasil from the German words. Before casting, the separate cylinder liners of highly wear-resistant silicon were placed in the foundry moulds and the aluminium alloy poured around them. The result was a cylinder bore that had far less internal friction and wear, with the added benefit of improved fuel economy. The cast-aluminium pistons had a thin iron coating applied to their outer (rubbing) surface. This development took place in collaboration with the specialist industry supplier Kolbenschmidt in Neckarsulm, some 20 miles to the north of Stuttgart.

A blend of ex-944 and ex-928 engine know-how saw the 3-litre dohc in-line four share many components with the 928 V8. It was the first Porsche engine to feature VarioCam.

Engines for the Future

The rather cramped space behind the cockpit meant that the engineers had to rethink the package. The exhaust system is bulky because it has to accommodate catalytic converters as well as dispel huge quantities of heat and meet both noise emission requirements and the exhaust sound that Porsche owners demand.

The VarioCam system was developed for the 968 engine. Operating on the inlet camshaft, it improved the running characteristics of the engine and at the same time lowered emissions and gave better cold starting.

The pistons were connected to the crankshaft by forged steel connecting rods that had had their big ends laser etched and then 'cracked' for a precise join when the bearing shells were inserted and the rod bolted together over the crankshaft. This process was a world first using forged rods, the process previously being possible only with sintered connecting rods.

Unique to the new family of engines was a special aluminium and grey cast-iron housing for the seven main-bearing forged crankshafts, in which were cast the bearing seats. In the same housing was the auxiliary shaft that drives the camshafts. This clever solution minimized stresses and temperature variations on the bearings and significantly reduced mechanical noise from the engine by its vibration damping effect. From the beginning of production the 986 engine's bearing carrier was different from that in the larger 996 engine, but from the summer of 1999 all engines shared the more robust 996 carrier.

Dual overhead camshafts were employed for each cylinder head (thereby making the

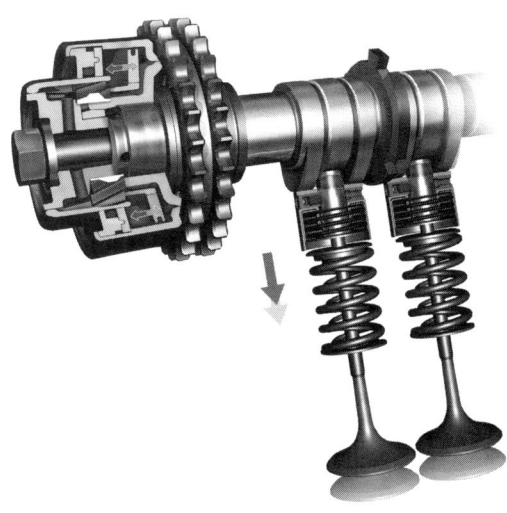

A further development of the company's renowned VarioCam system, it optimized power and torque outputs while reducing fuel consumption and exhaust gas emissions.

Engines for the Future

This graphic illustration shows the location of the components of the VarioCam system.

Boxster engine a 'quad-cam' unit) and were chain-driven off a countershaft positioned directly below the crankshaft and chain-driven by it at the ratio of 2:1. The countershaft had a gear sprocket at either end driving by chain the exhaust camshaft on each cylinder head. A shorter secondary chain drove the inlet camshaft.

This seemingly complex system is made possible by two features of the engine's design: the cylinder bores are slightly offset in relation to each other; and each cylinder head casting is identical. The chain drive mechanism therefore occupies the space at the front left for the left-hand cylinder bank and at the right rear for the right-hand cylinder bank. Each camshaft runs directly in machined surfaces in the head casting. There are two inlet valves of 33.3mm diameter and two exhaust valves of 28.1mm diameter for each cylinder with automatic hydraulic adjustment of the bucket tappet clearance. The chains are also automatically hydraulically tensioned to promote quiet operation at all engine speeds and a long, reliable service life.

Naturally the flow of gases through the combustion chamber is crossflow – the inlet system is located on top of the engine, the three-branch exhaust manifolds are underneath – with a single spark plug positioned centrally in the combustion chamber.

VarioCam

Developed for the water-cooled Porsche 968 engine was Porsche's VarioCam system that continuously monitors the timing of the inlet valves. With the new generation of engines it was natural that this sophisticated system be improved and incorporated in their design. Depending on throttle opening and engine load, the variance can be as much as 12.5 degrees advance or retard. This allows for better filling of the combustion chamber, more complete burning of the fuel and therefore greater control over hydrocarbon emissions. It also allows a broader, flatter torque curve and improves cold-start emissions.

The first Boxster engine (2.5 litres) was as compact as an engine can be given today's engineering requirements. It occupies far less space than an in-line engine, for example.

From its inception, the Porsche 911 engine featured a dry sump lubrication system. A scavenge pump pumped oil from an external storage tank (located in the engine compartment) to the vital components in the engine. This same sophistication has been carried over to the 986 engine, but with a twist – for the new engine it is what Porsche describes as an 'integrated' system, in which the oil tank is integrated into the lower part of the engine's cylinder block but kept separate to eliminate contamination and external hoses. It is also baffled to prevent starvation of vital engine components during high-G cornering activities. This simplification has undoubtedly saved Porsche on production costs.

When the engine is operating, oil is drawn from the tank by an engine-driven pump and distributed to the many points where it is needed in the engine and then returned to the tank by a scavenge pump. A thermostat and an oil/coolant heat exchanger monitor oil temperature and during the warm-up phase the system warms the oil directly from the coolant. This means that the engine reaches its normal operating temperature far more quickly. Whenever the oil temperature exceeds that of the coolant (about 90° C) under load, the heat exchanger process is reversed with the oil dissipating heat to the coolant.

Engines for the Future

Water-Cooling Arrives

But by far the most dramatic and significant change for Porsche has been the adoption of water-cooling instead of air-cooling in order to meet the new emission and noise regulations. One of the aims of the cooling system was to achieve consistent cylinder temperatures no matter how hard the engine was working. This was important in complete combustion of the fuel mixture and subsequently meeting ever-tightening emission requirements. The coolant is pumped around the engine and then through underbody piping to the angled front-mounted twin radiators before returning to the engine. The radiators are angled to minimize the amount of space that they consume in a very tight package, and to minimize their intrusion into the front luggage compartment.

As with all sophisticated modern high-performance engines today, the management of the fuel intake and an electronic module monitors exhaust gas systems. In the case of the 986 engine (and 996), it is the Bosch Motronic M5.2 system. The incoming air flows past a hot-film mass-metering unit inside the throttle body and into the combustion chambers, the fuel being injected in precise amounts into the intake manifold just upstream of the inlet valve. The actual intake manifold is a lightweight reinforced plastic moulding with extremely smooth internal surfaces to minimize internal air drag.

The exhaust gases are directed out of the cylinders to two stainless steel exhaust manifolds that are of tuned length with respect to each other, through two metal-based catalytic converters, each with an oxygen sensor, then to the muffler and then out into the atmosphere through that oh-so-sexy central exhaust pipe. As Ing Ulrich Schempp, who declares one of his hobbies as driving Boxsters, said:

> The packaging of the exhaust system posed a particularly difficult task for the engineers as they were confined in how much space was available to them. Not only that, but it was very important that

The exterior dimensions of the more powerful 3.2 Boxster S engine are almost the same as its smaller capacity sibling. The pity is that the engine is not visible to owners as it's hidden under the rear luggage compartment.

Engines for the Future

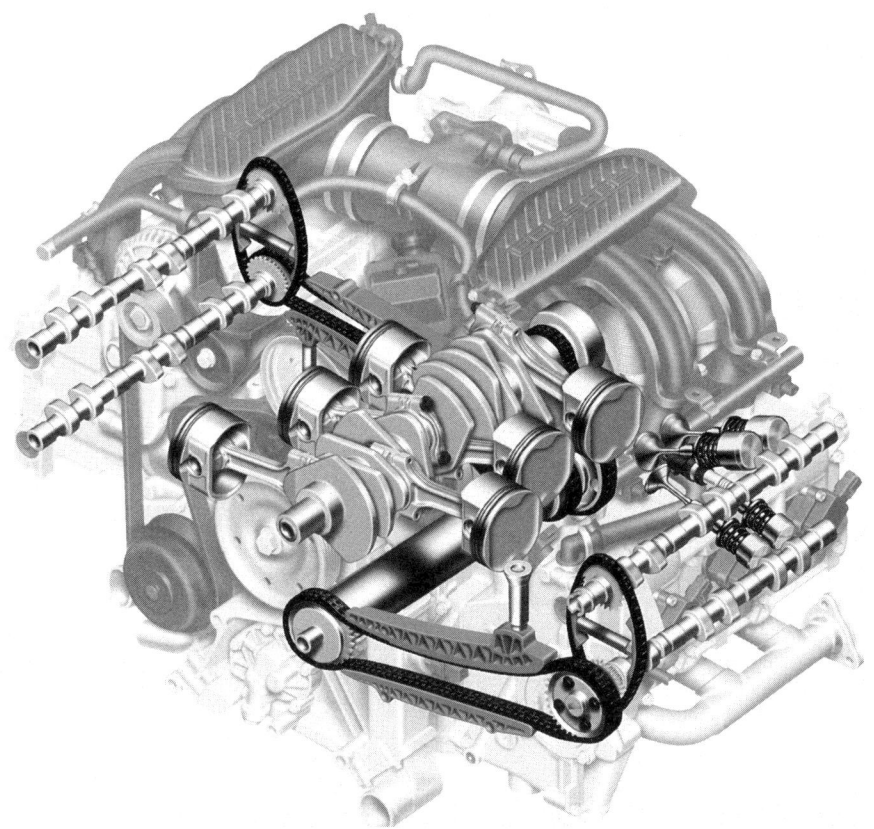

Porsche engineers developed an ingenious system to drive the four overhead camshafts of the Boxster engine. The flat, off-set layout of the engine allowed a drive system at each end, each a mirror image of the other.

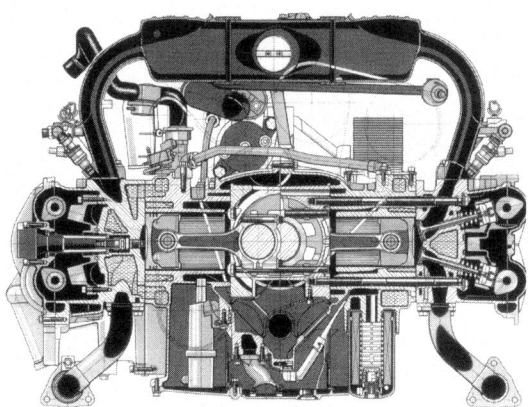

An interesting line drawing for those who appreciate the inner workings of a superb engine. This is the original 2.5 litre version.

Never afraid to innovate where engines are concerned, Porsche's engine designers devised a central 'cage' to accommodate the crankshaft and bearings. The layout of the valve train is also evident here.

Engines for the Future

Left *For technophiles who want to know the inside story, Porsche has published this magnificent technical cutaway drawing of its 986 engine.*

Opposite *With the coming of the 986 and 996 Porsche dramatically invested in new production technologies. However, the engine assembly was still largely the responsibility of a few skilled people.*

we got the acoustics of the exhaust right, that we achieved that certain sound that Porsche owners and enthusiasts expect from a flat-six Porsche engine.

The task was exacerbated by the need to comply with ever tightening noise pollution regulations. Retaining the Boxster concept car's central exhaust outlet actually gave Porsche some breathing space, not much but enough.

Boxster Specifics

The Boxster's ignition system is fully electronic with solid-state distribution of the current to six individual coils over each spark plug. The system naturally features cylinder-specific anti-knock control and automatic adjustment of the timing for specific cylinders. The system also includes a compensation capability that allows the engine to run quite satisfactorily on varying grades of fuel with minimal performance loss and no damage to the engine. It also features cylinder-selective anti-knock control that retards the ignition timing of individual cylinders that are about to knock. Second generation On-Board Diagnostics (OBD II) are incorporated for the North American market.

By the very nature of its mid-engined configuration servicing the Boxster was always going to be awkward so far as access was concerned. For the everyday needs, like checking the oil and water levels, the solution was simple. Under the rear hood, in the right hand corner, is a recess with three items: the engine coolant level is a visual check of the plastic expansion container that has a blue cap which unscrews if topping up is necessary; the actual dip stick has a yellow ring handle and if topping up is required that is done through the neck of the yellow-capped filler. In addition,

for the all-important oil level, it is displayed on a gauge in the instrument cluster each time the engine is started.

Major servicing must be done from underneath, although it must be said that the timing chains and poly-V belts that drive the alternator, water pump, hydraulic pump and air-conditioning compressor all feature automatic tensioning and are basically maintenance-free.

For the original version of the Boxster, the only engine on offer was a 2.5-litre version of the six-cylinder engine that was a part of the new family. With a cylinder bore of 85.5mm and a crank stroke of 72.0mm, its capacity was 2,480cc. Power output was a very respectable 204bhp at 6,000rpm and 181lb ft of torque at 4,500rpm on a compression ratio of 11.0:1. Amazingly for such a sports oriented engine, some 147lb ft of torque was available from between 1,750 to 6,400rpm. Its specific output was an excellent 81.6bhp per litre.

As with any new Porsche product, this was only the beginning of a long period of steady development that would see significant increases in capacity in the future.

5 Hidden Pleasures

For technophiles, Porsches have always made excellent reading. The company's engineers have embraced interesting, and indeed often unique, solutions to the various technical problems that beset an automotive engineer. And the 986 is no exception. The solutions chosen to suspend the Boxster, both front and rear, as well as the steering gear, the gearboxes and braking system are all extremely elegant and a delight to the eye of those for whom such mechanical elegance is important.

Prototype Testing

But there is a far less glamorous, although fascinating nonetheless, aspect of building desirable sports cars and that is prototype testing. Development of the mechanical package began before hand-built 986 bodies were available, the 'mules' being 911s that had been converted to the mid-engined configuration and the aluminium-intensive suspension system. As development and durability testing

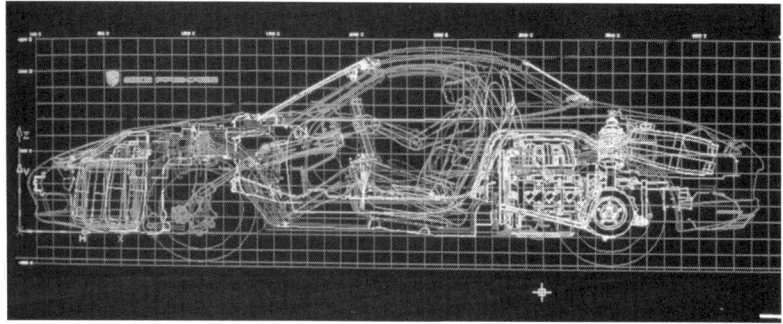

A computer model of the Boxster and the location of its components, a difficult task for the designers.

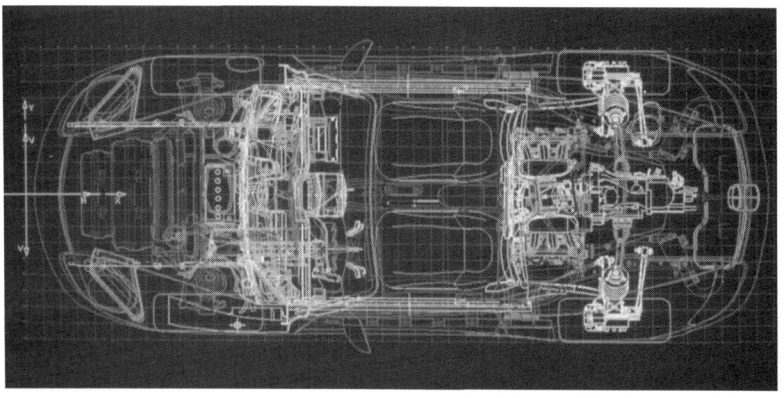

A plan view of the disposition of components within the Porsche Boxster.

Hidden Pleasures

Ouch! An expensive hand-built prototype Boxster being destroyed in the name of scientific research against an offset barrier.

progressed, these Phase I cars were upgraded. These vehicles had no gurney flap and a higher rear end, but they served to validate the basic technical solutions, crash requirements and service stability.

With the success of the Boxster concept car the styling was reworked and a series of Phase II prototypes was built that incorporated all the lessons learned in Phase I. In styling, these Phase II cars resembled the later series production cars.

The extremely rigid body structure had been built using hot-galvanized steel. While Porsche engineers have a vast storehouse of experience and expertise with aluminium alloys as a body material, as well as expensive high-tech composites, steel was chosen for the Boxster on the

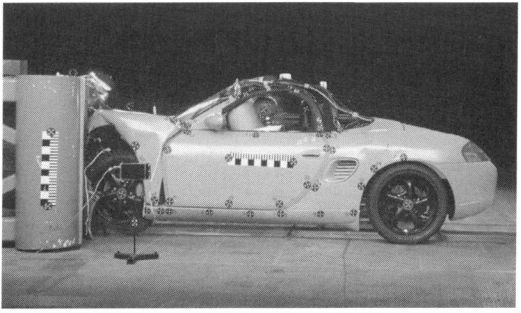

As well as the offset test, the Boxster underwent full frontal, side and rollover tests to prove the computer calculations and to ensure compliance with the toughest legal requirements.

grounds of superior deformation performance, cost and simplicity of repair. Mundane perhaps, but practical. Integrated into the front and rear structures were zones of deformation designed to 'give' in a scientifically calculated manner in

Hidden Pleasures

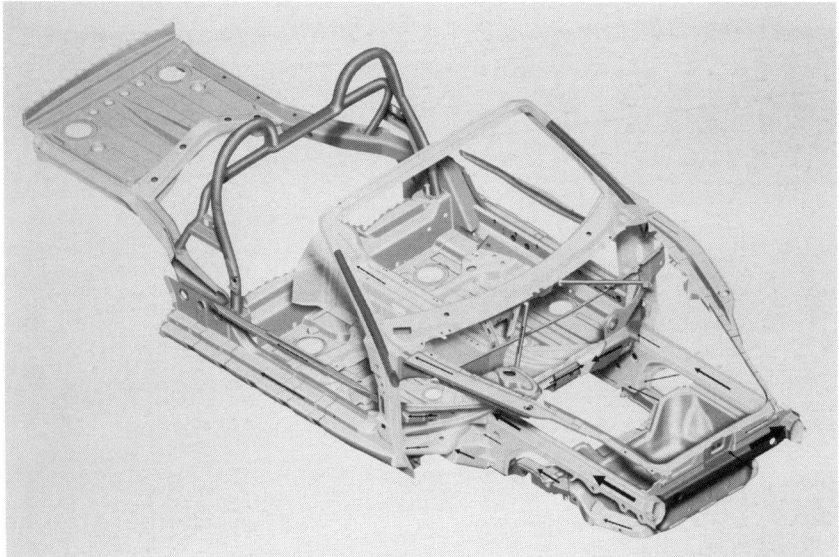

Porsche engineers have provided immensely strong reinforced steel A-pillars as well as rollover hoops behind the seats.

the event of an accident. The design of the frontal structure was common to both the 986 and 996 Porsches and, apart from collapsing to absorb the energy of impact, dissipated it around the passenger cell.

Greater body stability, with minimal weight penalty, was arrived at by using high-strength steel body panels reinforced where necessary from both computer simulations and real-world crash tests carried out on prototypes. For example, the side-impact beams in the doors as well as the reinforcement of the bulkhead cross-member were made from a super-strong steel/boron alloy formed to shape under high temperatures.

Welded into the structure, behind the occupant's seats and as part of the windscreen frame, were high-strength steel rollover hoops designed to protect the occupants should the unexpected ever occur.

According to Ing Ulrich Schempp:

> The Weissach engineers devoted thousands of hours of vital computer time to carrying out simulations on the Boxster's structure to refine its capabilities to deform and to absorb the enormous amounts of energy generated in a high speed impact; to ensure that the car's occupants were protected as much as possible; and to ensure that all current and future legislative requirements were met or exceeded. For example, the front-end structure is manufactured using high-strength steel panels and has been patented by the company.

Airbags were provided for each occupant in addition to their seat belts and the built-in protection from the body.

Hard/Soft-Top

Roadsters are great fun in sunny weather. A sudden change should not spoil the driving fun and so Porsche engineers designed and developed in conjunction with Car Top Systems, a joint venture company with Daimler-Chrysler for whom it also makes the folding metal hardtop for the SLK model, two roofs: a folding convertible hood and a detachable hardtop. The convertible hood presented two potential problems for the designers: ease and speed of folding/raising, and noise levels when cruising with it raised.

Hidden Pleasures

Porsche designers and engineers have devised a completely new Z-fold system for the Boxster's soft-top that is far smaller in volume when folded; from top up to top down takes only 12sec.

Hidden Pleasures

It was not all plain sailing during the development process, as Schempp explained:

> The convertible top for the Boxster was a totally new development with a new motion sequence that had never been used before. At first we tried to activate the movement of the top and the compartment lid with a lever to the left of the driver's seat. The manual force needed to make it work was very high at first so that ever more money had to be sunk into high-grade Bowden cables and the propulsion system.
>
> These requirements made the mechanical convertible top operation more expensive, so that in the end there was no great difference in price from an electrical operation. Taking the demands of comfort into account an electrical top operation is preferable and so at a relatively late stage it was decided to change over to the electrical drive system.

The convertible roof is a clever and elegant piece of engineering, something you would expect from Porsche. The support bars are cast magnesium and therefore light and strong. After unfastening the central catch on the windscreen header rail, the operator then presses a button, an electric motor whirs and the whole ensemble folds down beneath a flap in just 12sec. Conversely, raising it also requires only 12sec.

Interestingly, before the Boxster went into production the International Magnesium Agency in Ube, Japan, conferred a design award on the Boxster's roof.

For those owners who prefer it, an aluminium hardtop is also available. Weighing a mere 55lb (25kg), it provides more insulation than the convertible roof, is quieter when cruising even though the soft-top has spent many hours in the Weissach wind tunnel where noise levels were reduced significantly compared with other soft-tops, and has an electric demister in the rear glass.

Suspension

Primary safety, or active safety as many like to refer to it, has always been at the top of the priority list with any Porsche and the 986 is no exception. Compared with its co-development sibling, the 996, the packaging requirements were both similar and different: the front suspension is, for the most part, common between the two new Porsches; however, the rear suspension is different in the details reflecting the different packaging brought about by their differing engine positions (mid versus rear) and space requirements. With the Boxster the weight distribution was near the ideal 50:50. Factor in the car's low centre of gravity and long wheelbase (relative to its overall length) and the potential should be obvious.

Porsche has a long history of using torsion bars as its suspension medium – the 911 had used them, as had the 356. However, their days had passed, as Schempp explained:

To safeguard the lives of many drivers, Porsche has developed its stability management system (PSM) that electronically manages the engine's power delivery depending on speed and other factors. For the brave, it can be switched off.

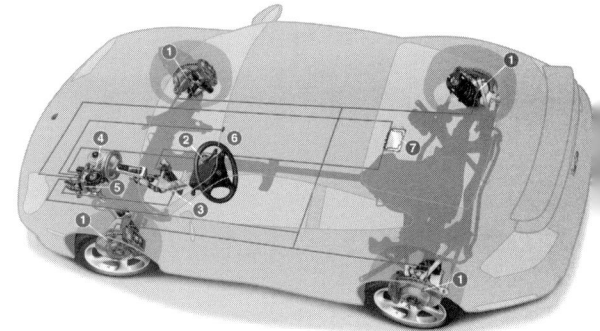

Hidden Pleasures

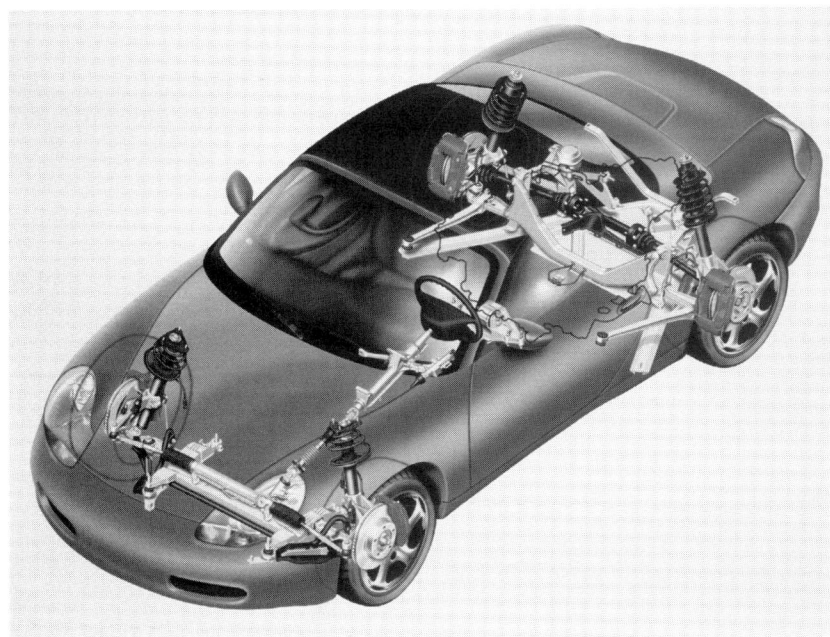

An artist's view of the sophisticated running gear of the Boxster.

The torsion bar suspension is definitely an ingenious solution and has done a good job in Porsche vehicles for many years. But there were packaging advantages available to us by moving to coil springs, and they offered many more possibilities for implementing a progressive spring characteristic, thus achieving a more favourable relationship between sportiness and comfort, and we could improve the cushioning behaviour to again achieve comfort advantages.

The front suspension utilizes the ubiquitous MacPherson struts with coil springs that are conical in shape (they are much wider at their base compared with their top) and twin-tube gas pressure dampers. The strut is attached to a die-cast aluminium wheel hub that is in turn connected to an A-arm lower wishbone (also made from aluminium) via a ball joint.

The suspension assembly and the forward-mounted steering rack (positioned forward of the front wheel's centre line) are mounted on an I-shaped cast aluminium subframe that is bolted to the underbody at four rubber-insulated points. These provide exact geometric location of the subframe and also filter out unwanted noise, vibration and harshness (NVH).

The Boxster's MacPherson strut-type front suspension features forged aluminium lower wishbones, aluminium die-cast hub and subframe.

Hidden Pleasures

The aluminium intensive rear suspension is attached to a deep and rigid cast aluminium subframe.

In basic layout the 986's independent rear suspension is very similar to that at the front. The coil springs over the struts are again conical, although they now have two more winds in each spring and again die-cast wheel hubs are specified. Location of each rear wheel is by way of two forged aluminium lateral links – one in front of the wheel's centre line, the other behind – and a single trailing link.

There is a far more substantial cast aluminium subframe at the rear that is bolted up to the underbody. It is larger because it not only has to support the suspension system but also the engine-transmission assembly.

At both ends transverse torsion stabilizer bars are attached to the hub carriers by rubber-insulated linkages. The front bar is 23.1mm in diameter while the rear is 18.5mm. However, if you order the Sports Suspension package the bars will be increased in diameter to 23.6mm and 19.6mm front and rear respectively, together with slightly firmer springs and damper settings.

Originally developed for the 928 was what Porsche engineers termed the 'Weissach' axle.

It was a particularly clever piece of engineering that varied the geometry of the links guiding each rear wheel, promoting what the company referred to as active rear steering. The mounting points for the suspension linkages permitted small but significant variations in toe-in during cornering to counteract oversteer tendencies. The buzzword at the time was 'elastokinematics'. Mazda and Honda actually engineered and produced complex and costly rear wheel steering systems to achieve basically the same ends.

The Boxster has inherited a variation on the original system and through subtle changes in the toe-in or toe-out attitude of the wheels under load will improve the car's stability and promote understeer characteristics in preference to oversteer. The suspension's geometry provides a negative toe position on the outer front wheel in a bend and under lateral forces, the outer rear wheel develops a positive toe-in position. With increased transverse acceleration this deliberately increases the car's understeer. It also allows the driver to brake when cornering and maintain full control of the car.

Hidden Pleasures

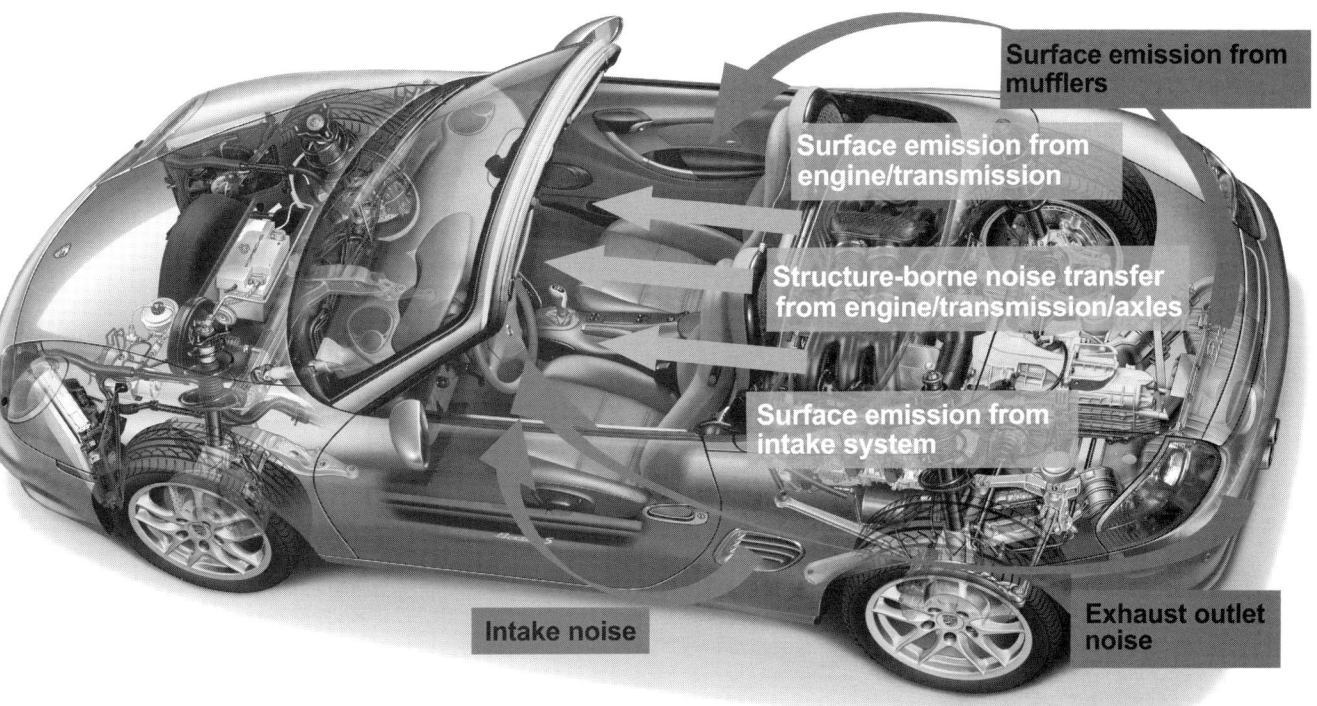

In any roadster the occupants are going to be assailed by far more noise than in a saloon. By careful management of these noise paths the distraction can be significantly reduced.

Steering

All Porsches since the original 911 have been fitted with a rack and pinion steering system and even though there is no engine positioned between the front wheels of a Boxster, the company's engineers still opted to fit power steering. Apparently several prototypes were not fitted with power steering and the drivers reported excellent feedback and precision with little increased effort, but, nevertheless, a marketing decision was made to fit assistance and avoid any potential dissatisfaction from owners. The Boxster's steering system is hydraulically powered (rather than electrically powered as on the MG F and TF as well as the Honda S2000 and BMW Z4), but still retains good feedback to the rim of the steering wheel.

The overall steering ratio is 16.9:1 that gives three turns lock-to-lock of the rake and reach adjustable airbag equipped steering wheel.

Brakes

Four-wheel discs provide braking for the Boxster, each disc being internally ventilated and clamped by a monobloc four-pot aluminium caliper with the name PORSCHE proudly prominent. This technology was first proved in the Group C Porsche 956 and is also used in Formula 1. The discs at the front are 292mm in diameter by 24mm thick, while those at the rear are 290mm by 20mm and

The Boxster has a powerful four-wheel ventilated disc braking system with four-pot callipers at the front.

incorporate a small 164mm diameter by 20mm wide drum for the emergency handbrake. Keeping brakes cooled in the heat of sports car driving is important. With the Boxster's system Porsche engineers have provided two incoming streams of air: from the front spoiler and additional air directed to the disc rotors via 'guide spoilers' on the suspension control arms.

Transmission

The engine's power is delivered to the rear wheels through one of two gearboxes on offer. Traditionalists demand a manual gearbox and that for the Boxster is a five speeder designed by Porsche but developed and manufactured in conjunction with long-time associates Volkswagen. Gear shifts are made by a cable-operated mechanism rather than a shaft linkage because of the position of the gearshift relative to the gearbox. The positions for the first four gears conform to the standard H pattern, with fifth to the right and up, reverse being slightly further to the right and down so as not to be directly below fifth.

The clutch is a single dry plate unit with hydraulic actuation.

Buyers who select the automatic gearbox option receive the Tiptronic S five-speed automatic that was developed by Porsche in conjunction with the specialist transmission manufacturer ZF in Friedrichshafen. The Tiptronic electronic control unit allows a great deal of flexibility in the way in which the gearbox can be used, far more so than with the similarly equipped Porsche 911, for example. If you simply want to drive from A to B you could select 'D' for drive and the gearshifts would take place smoothly with no further input from the driver.

However, if you feel in the mood for sporting driving, you simply push the selector across the gate to the 'M' position and the maps in the control module take over and let the driver control each gearshift. The shifts from one gear to the next are made by pushing either the '+' button on the steering wheel to move up a gear, or by pressing the '-' button to drop down a gear; two presses to drop down two gears. An override in the ECU protects the engine from overrevving if the driver accidentally presses the '-' button and if, at that moment it is likely to exceed the engine's safe rev limit, will not allow the gear to be selected.

Similarly, the ECU will not shift up a gear if the driver presses the '+' button mid-corner. There are more features, however, all designed to increase the enjoyment and safety of driving. The Boxster's system goes far beyond acceleration management and can (and will) make logical decisions about the appropriate gear. If, for example, the driver takes his foot

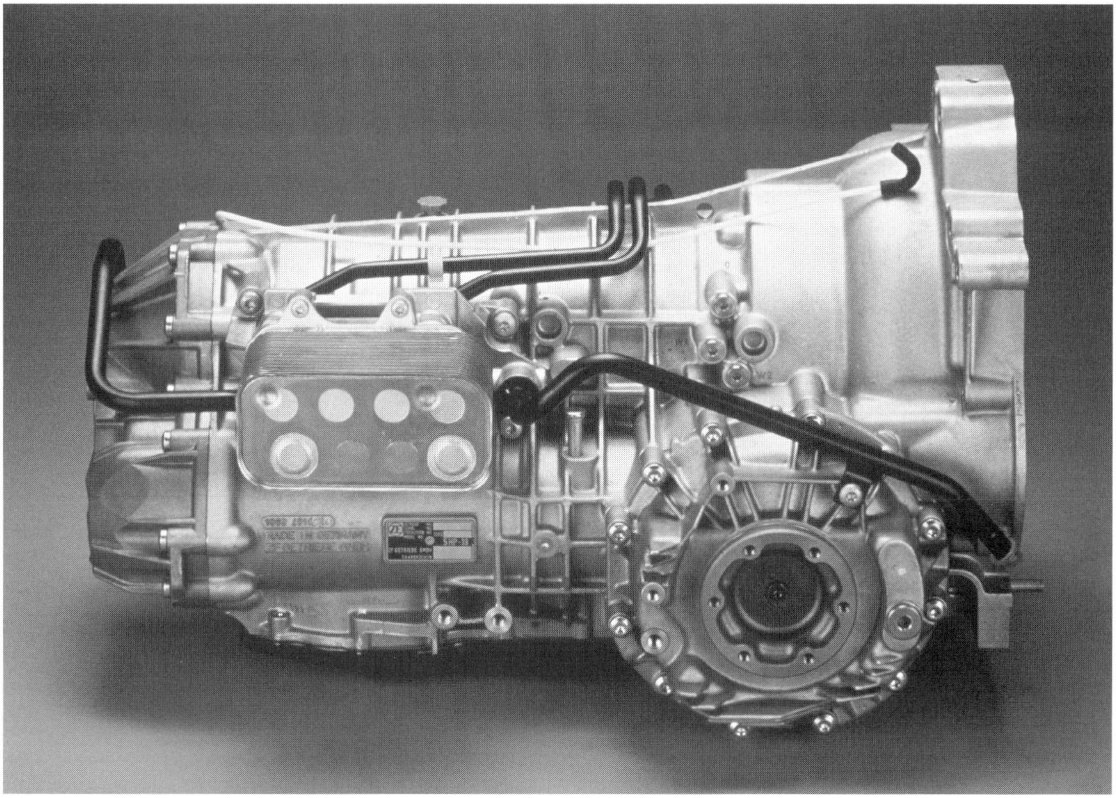

Hidden Pleasures

German gearbox specialist ZF supplies Porsche with its five-speed Tiptronic S gearbox.

In collaboration with VW, Porsche developed a new five-speed manual gearbox for the Boxster; gear selection was via cables and not the usual rod and linkage method.

Hidden Pleasures

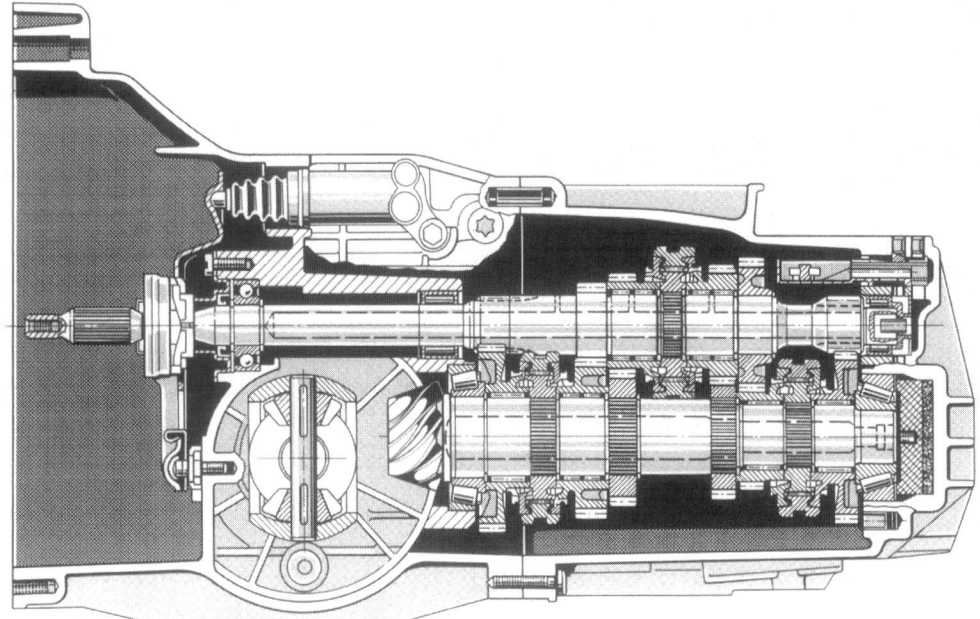

A completely new 5-speed manual gearbox was developed for the Boxster, a gearbox that has proven capable of accepting far more power than the standard 2.5 litre engine could deliver.

off the accelerator, as when approaching a bend, the electronic module will sense that the car is no longer under power and will prevent the transmission from changing up a gear (or two). Braking will cause the transmission to drop back a gear when the appropriate road speed has been reached, ready for powering out of a corner. On slippery surfaces the system will change up earlier than normal to minimize wheel spin.

An option is traction control that extends throughout the Boxster's full speed range by combining with Porsche's automatic brake differential (ABD) that reduces power when wheel spin is detected regardless of speed. Of course, if the driver so desires, the throttle override can be cancelled by switching off the traction control; the ABD remains active.

The standard wheels for the Boxster are a forged aluminium five-spoke design, 16 × 6 at the front and 16 × 7 at the rear shod with 205/55 ZR16 tyres on the front and 225/50 ZR16 at the rear. If you preferred to tick the Sports Suspension box on the order form the wheels and tyres go to 1in in diameter, 17 × 7 with 205/50 ZR17 at the front and 17 × 8.5 with 255/40 ZR17 at the rear. In the UK, 17in wheels are the most popular.

Only in the USA! A prototype Boxster is escorted out of town by a posse riding Harleys.

Hidden Pleasures

Above *Arctic conditions did not faze the Boxster, although the Porsche test engineers might not have been convinced!*

Below *Boxster prototypes were tested under the most gruelling of conditions in many secret locations.*

6 Looking at the Market

Where all previous attempts by Porsche to market a more affordable sports car had been linked to Volkswagen – the 914 and 924 – the new model would be exclusively Porsche. The decision was made from the outset that the new sports car would a genuine Porsche embodying all the DNA characteristics that implied.

The aim of the company was to produce a sports car that would appeal to a far wider audience than hitherto and one that would 'win the hearts of more women drivers', as Wendelin Wiedeking said on more than one occasion. The target group was people in the thirty-five to forty years age bracket, around ten years younger than a typical 911 buyer.

From the late 1970s through to the late

For many years the only open-air Porsches were the 911 and 944/968 cabrios, but they were rather exclusive. The Boxster was a new deal for Porsche enthusiasts who wanted wind-in-the-hair motoring.

1980s interest in sports cars, and indeed sports coupés, waned dramatically in virtually all markets. Only the manufacturers catering to the upper end of the market continued to offer both body types through this barren period. Mercedes-Benz, Ferrari and Porsche were the notable stayers, while a little further down the socio-economic scale the likes of Fiat, Alfa Romeo and most of the Japanese manufacturers quietly faded from the scene. Many critics have put forward various theories about the phenomenon, but the most likely scenario was that buyers were disenchanted with the poor selection that was on offer – most coupés were simply re-roofed two-door sedans and what soft-top roadsters were available were generally British and v-e-r-y long in the tooth. The MG range, for example, was a sad reflection of what was wrong with the industry and much the same was happening in Italy at Fiat where the 124-based Spider hung around long after its use-by date, and its replacement, the X1/9, filled a completely different niche in the market. The Alfa Romeo 2000 Spider was kept in production for more than two decades and was to suffer more facial and rear-end transplants than one of Hollywood's aging stars! From the buyer's point of view, they were all just a bit passé.

Mazda MX-5

The 1990s saw a great revival in open-topped sports cars following the sales success of the Mazda MX-5 that was first shown at the Chicago Motor Show in 1989 and released in Japan in late 1989. Unashamedly inspired by

When on a good thing, stick to it; and Mazda did with the Mark II, which was an even more successful roadster for the innovative Japanese company. (Photograph courtesy of Mazda)

Looking at the Market

Colin Chapman's epochal Lotus Élan that he began selling in the mid-1960s, the MX-5 re-awakened the dormant desire in many 'baby boomers' to break away from their staid, conventional sedans and station wagons and rekindle that wind-in-the-hair exhilaration that only a roadster can provide. Mazda cleverly mixed the nostalgic with the new in their sports car, as did Chapman: the 1.6-litre engine was based on a 323 sedan engine but further developed with a dohc cylinder head and various tuning tweaks to produce 110bhp of power at 6,500rpm and 100lb ft of torque at 5,500rpm; the body was essentially a self-supporting monocoque, but had a massive cast aluminium vertical 'ladder' running the length of the underbody tunnel connecting the engine/gearbox assembly to the differential to provide extra rigidity for both the body structure and the driveline; and the multi-link fully independent a suspension system that was unique in Mazdaworld to the MX-5. The parallels with the Élan were undeniable and uncanny. A model upgrade in 1993 and a more powerful 128bhp 1.8-litre engine kept the momentum well and truly going for Mazda. Performance was always keen for its size, the 1.6 MX-5 being capable of a 0–60mph time of 9.7sec and a maximum of 119mph (192km/h). The 1.8 improved on those figures, reducing the 0–60mph time to 8.5sec and running to 127mph (204km/h). In England BBR offered a turbo kit that upped the power to 150bhp at 6,500rpm, torque to 154lb ft at 5,500rpm and brought the 0–60mph time back to 7.8sec.

The Australians even made their own manic limited edition turbocharged version – the MX-5 SP – that knocked out 204bhp of power and an enormous 280 Nm of torque for a 0–100km/h time of 6.3sec and a maximum speed of 140mph (225km/h)!

In 1998 Mazda released the thoroughly revised Mark II version, which neatly retained the essence of the original's classic styling.

Both 1.6- and 1.8-litre engines were on offer. Power for the 1.6 remained at 110bhp at 6,500rpm with maximum torque coming in at 5,000, while for the 1.8 its power was rated at 146bhp at a heady 7,000rpm. Their on-road performance was line ball with the earlier editions.

MG

After a brief hesitation – it was almost as if the rest of the world's manufacturers had been caught with their collective pants down – several others flocked into the previously untapped market segment. Rover entered with its MG F that was shown at Geneva in March 1995 and, somewhat radically perhaps, configured as a mid-engined sports car (how prescient was that?). Power came from two versions of the excellent K-Series 1.8 aluminium alloy four-cylinder engine: the plain 1.8 developed 120bhp at 5,500rpm and 122lb ft of torque at 3,000rpm, while the high performance version with Variable Valve Control (VVC) developed 145bhp at 7,000rpm and 128lb ft at 4,500rpm. Despite having only 1.8 litres behind the driver, the MG F could zip from rest to 60mph in 8.5sec and run to 120mph, while the VVC version would sprint from 0–60mph in 7sec and had a top speed of 130mph (209km/h).

The MG F's suspension system was naturally fully independent, though not by conventional springs as might have been expected, but by a further developed version of Alex Moulton's excellent Hydragas® system. This provided the little sports car with a near ideal compromise between ride and handling. As for the styling, it was evocative of several stillborn styling studies that emanated from the disastrous British Leyland period of ownership of the famous octagon badge. The MG F quickly became the best-selling sports car in Europe with more than 77,000 being built.

In January 2002 it was upgraded signifi-

Above and Left *Like Mazda, MG upgraded the MG F significantly without changing all the good things that made the original so popular. In many ways, the MG TF is a baby Boxster. (Photograph courtesy of MG Rover)*

Looking at the Market

cantly to the point where MG-Rover liked to think of it as a new model in its own right – strengthened body structure and a completely new suspension system utilizing coil springs and wishbones that has biased the car's characteristics more towards the handling side of the ledger with some (but not a lot) sacrifice to the ride. The MG TF, as it was badged, came in a variety of specifications from the plain 1.6-litre 115, so named because that was the K-Series engine's output in bhp; the 120 for the same reason; the 135 and the storming 160 that boasted no less than 160bhp out of the all-alloy engine. Performance varied from a 0–60mph time of 9.2sec for the 115 through to a very quick 6.9sec for the 160, top speeds ranging from 118–mph (189–220km/h).

The MG TF is selling strongly in England and Europe with solid increases in sales in Asia and Australia.

Toyota's Contribution

Toyota, never one to miss out on somebody else's good fortune, muscled in with the dumpy-looking Targa-topped MR2 released in Japan in mid-1984 and in the UK in March 1985. Based on Corolla mechanical components in a unique body, the mid-engined sports car quickly gained a reputation for handling quirks and, apart from the huge Japanese market, was not particularly successful in the export markets. The 4A-GE engine, otherwise known as the 1.6-litre twin-cam 16V Corolla GT engine, was good for 130bhp at 6,600rpm and pushed the little MR2 to a top speed in the region of 130mph (209km/h) with a 0–60mph time of 7.7sec. This was replaced in 1989 by the Ferrari lookalike MR2 that again used mostly off-the-shelf Corolla bits and pieces. It was available with either a naturally

The MR2 had a slow start in the world, but the Boxster clone-like model of today has brought recognition to the company. It is very light and the ride is hard, but it handles brilliantly. (Photograph courtesy of Toyota GB)

Looking at the Market

The new Spider brought renewed confidence to Alfa Romeo and new buyers who wanted Italian style and brio. The V6 version is very quick. (Photograph courtesy of Fiat Group)

aspirated or turbo engine – the 3S-GTE of 1,998cc capacity with an output of 225bhp, although was never an official UK import. Sales began in April 1990 with the naturally aspirated engine that gave 158bhp at 6,600rpm. This MR2 was far more successful, although the Turbo version was tricky to handle on the limits.

In 2000 a complete model change took place and the latest MR2 hit the market looking for all the world like a sanforized Boxster but with the smoothness of the Porsche's lines swapped for angular lines that don't gel in the way that perhaps Toyota intended. Power now came from a VVT-i version of the Corolla dohc 1.8-litre in-line four-cylinder engine (the 1ZZ-FE) that is, like it has been in all MR2s, mounted transversely behind the passenger compartment. Power output is an impressive 138bhp. An unusual refinement available as an option on the new MR2 is the sequential automatic gearbox that could be used with either the steering wheel buttons or by flicking the floor lever whenever the driver wants to change gears. The electronics that control the system thoughtfully include a facility to 'blip' the accelerator on down-changes to smooth out the change and take some pressure off the driveline.

While the handling is go-kart-like in its directness and responsiveness, the lightweight body does not inspire confidence and the ride from the all-independent suspension is very hard and unforgiving to the point of being tiring after the first few miles of a drive. Still, it is nippy, running 0–60mph on 8.0sec and a maximum speed of 129mph (208km/h).

Alfa Romeo and Fiat

Alfa Romeo, until its near downfall in the 1980s before being rescued by the giant FIAT Group in 1986, was a world-renowned maker of sports cars as exemplified by the Giulietta and Giulia Sprint followed by the Duetto in 1966 that morphed into the long-running 1600/1750/2000 Spider, which lasted from the mid-1960s (remember Dustin Hoffman in *The Graduate*?) through to the early 1990s in various forms. The constants with all these Alfa sports cars were their glorious styling – Bertone did the Giulietta, Giulia, 1600/1750/2000 coupés, while Farina (later Pininfarina) drew and built the Spider versions of each – coupled to a spirited all-alloy dohc four-cylinder engine driving the rear wheels through a five-speed manual gearbox.

Looking at the Market

Long after the fondly remembered Fiat 124 Spider and X1/9 came the Barchetta that has been a steady seller for Fiat for several seasons because it is good value for money. (Photograph courtesy of Fiat Group)

Suspension was coils and wishbones at the front, live axle with coil springs at the rear. They were especially endearing cars to drive.

Following the demise of the 2000 Spider there was a lengthy hiatus in Alfa Romeo's sports car programme until 1994 when the current Alfa GTV and Spider were released. These 'twins' share Pininfarina styling – they had originally been displayed as concept cars – and share most body and mechanical components, a first for Alfa. But the most striking feature (apart from their glorious styling) of the new Spider (and GTV) is the use of front-wheel drive, a move forced on Alfa's engineers by the use of a Fiat Tipo-based floorpan. The suspension is fully independent by Alfa Romeo-designed multi-links and coil springs all round and the Fiat-based 2-litre in-line engine is a new development with dohc and sixteen-valves. Power is 150bhp for a 0–60mph time of 8.4sec and a maximum of 134mph (216km/h). Added to the range was the lusty 3.0-litre V6 Lusso version that improved the performance markedly – 0–60mph in 6.8sec, maximum of 154mph (248km/h) – and increased the aural enjoyment by a factor of at least tenfold.

Despite the front-wheel drive configuration, the new Alfa Romeo sports car has proven to be a big seller for the company. Rumours in the industry are suggesting that the Spider's (and GTV's) successor will return to the classic front engine/rear wheel drive configuration. I for one certainly hope so.

Fiat, too, fielded its Barchetta that was also based on the Punto Mark I floorpan (that has been out of production for four years!), transverse engine and transmission arrangement and unusual Chris Bangle-inspired body styling. Its 1.8-litre engine (from the same family as the Alfa Romeo's) developed 130bhp at 6,300rpm and can push it to a time of 8.9sec for the 0-60mph run and on to a maximum of 124mph. Available only in left-hand drive, it has been moderately successful but is now well passed its use-by date compared with most of its rivals although a recent facelift (nip and tuck really, new nose styling, brake light in the boot lid, big bore exhaust) and a price reduction have helped renew interest in it.

The Australian Ford

An unusual rival to the world-conquering Mazda MX-5 came from a most unlikely source – the Ford Motor Company of Australia – in the form of the Ford Capri, not to be confused with the 1960s British Ford of the same name. Ford had a business tie-up with Mazda selling rebadged Mazda 323s as Ford Lasers and 626s as Ford Telstars that were both very popular in Australia. By combining the talents of Ford's Ghia subsidiary in Turin to style its sports car (displayed as the Ford Barchetta at the various European motor shows in the mid-1980s) and the mechanical components from the popular front-wheel drive Mazda 323 with the undoubted abilities of its own engineers to get a job done on a shoestring budget, Ford figured it could build a sports car that would give it some cachet in the burgeoning sports car market. Introduced in late 1989, Ford offered normally aspirated (84bhp) and turbocharged (136bhp) 1.6-litre versions of the Capri and, after a few teething problems mainly to do with weather sealing of the convertible top, these sold steadily through the early 1990s in Australia, south-east Asia and through the Lincoln-Mercury dealers in America. In Australia the Capri outsold the Mazda MX-5 for most of its short lifespan – production ended in mid-1994.

The Australian response to the Mazda MX-5 was the Capri. Based on the floorpan of the Mazda 323, it was an unusual amalgam of input from various parts of the Ford Empire. The standard version was not that quick but the Turbo was. (Photograph courtesy of Ford Australia)

Fast forward to the twenty-first Century and Honda again breaks many of the rules with the S2000. Startling performance from just 2-litres, a distinctive style and brilliant roadholding even if the ride is a little harsh. (Photograph courtesy of Honda UK)

Small but Powerful Honda

In recent times Honda has re-entered the sports car market with its S2000, the company's first real sports car since the cute-and-collectible S500/S600/S800s of the 1960s. Powered by an all-new 2-litre in-line dohc all-alloy four-cylinder engine that uses Honda's Formula 1 developed VTEC valve system, the S2000 develops 240bhp of power at 8,300rpm – an astonishing 120bhp per litre – and 153lb ft of torque at 7,500rpm. It even qualifies for the strict Californian Low Emission Vehicle (LEV) and German D3 emission requirements. This gives the 1,260kg (2,778lb) roadster rocket-like performance capabilities, like a 0–100km/h time of 6.9sec and a maximum speed of 150mph (240km/h). The engine, often described in the media as the most sophisticated four-cylinder engine ever made, is a real screamer – it is red-lined on the tachometer at 9,000rpm! Like all Honda VTEC engines it fails to set the world alight at anything below 6,000rpm, but from there to the red-line it is transformed into a veritable kamikaze screamer. It is almost schizophrenic, so different are its two characters.

For the 2004 model year Honda released a thoroughly revised version that answered some of the criticisms of the original, notably the lack of mid-range torque. The new model has an engine of 2.2-litres capacity that accompanies revised suspension settings, new body detailing and a better six-speed manual gearbox. Although the engine is larger in capacity, its power output remains at 240bhp, but is now developed at a less manic 7,800rpm (down from 8,300rpm) and torque has been increased slightly to 161lb ft at 6,500rpm, a full 1,000rpm lower down the scale.

The gearbox's ratios are slightly longer in fifth and sixth gears for better cruising capabilities and the synchromesh has been improved to give the driver an even more pleasing gearshift movement. There's now a slightly firmer front end and the rear suspension ride height has been lowered a tad and the springs softened ever so slightly, while revised spoilers and side skirts make up the new appearance package. For those keen of eye, the only change inside is to the tachometer – the red-line has been brought back from 9,000rpm to a mere 8,200rpm.

The S2000s destined for England retained the earlier engine but included all the other improvements.

The car that saved the company. The Lotus Elise was a groundbreaker in true Lotus tradition – lightweight aluminium tub and mostly alloy components as well as a minimalist body to keep out most draughts. (Photograph courtesy of Lotus Cars)

Lotus Elise and the Vauxhall VX220

Out of left field in the sports car market, or roadster market as many would have it, can be listed two cars that are delightfully outrageous in comparison with their peers. They are the Lotus Elise and Vauxhall VX220. Both utilize a common technology that centres on lightweight aluminium castings and extrusions as the material for the construction of their punt-type platform, the various pieces being hydro-formed and bonded to make an immensely strong and rigid base for the suspension. And both are transverse mid-engined and exciting to drive. The Elise emerged from the Lotus works back in 1996 and caused a sensation at the time. Power comes from the same family of engines as that which powers the MG, the Rover K-Series. However, it has always been rated slightly higher in Lotus-spec. Combined with minimal weight (around 750kg (1,652lb)) and a racing-inspired suspension system the 122bhp Elise Roadster scoots from 0–60mph in 5.8sec while the more powerful 156bhp Elise 111 does it in 5.1sec. Top speeds are 125 and 132mph (200–212km/h) respectively.

Looking at the Market

For the 2004 model year, Lotus has added the Toyota Celica 1.8 VVT-i dohc engine that already meets the much more stringent American market emission requirements to the Elise range (it will power all US-destined Elises), while the K-Series engine remains for the UK and European markets.

Like Ford in Australia with the Capri, Vauxhall was always an unlikely producer of sports cars, having a history for most of its 100 years of making plain Jane humdrum family cars of dubious reliability and quality. But that notwithstanding, an important part of today's range of Vauxhall cars is the VX220, a mid-engined roadster that is based on the Lotus Elise technology. The aluminium intensive chassis of the VX220 is a direct result of a technical collaboration between Lotus and Vauxhall engineers; it's just slightly larger, that's all. Positioned immediately behind the driver/passenger is the Vectra in-line dohc engine available in two guises: 2.2i naturally aspirated and 2.0 Turbo. Power output is 145bhp and 200bhp respectively for 0–60mph acceleration times of 5.6 and 4.7sec and maximum speeds of 137mph (220km/h) and 151mph (243km/h). *CAR* magazine, in commenting on the VX220, said, 'In turbo guise no car is quicker for the money.'

Audi Enters the Sports Market

Audi, not a company with any post-war tradition where roadsters were concerned, was not to be left out of the burgeoning sports roadster market. It exhibited its TT concept car at the 1997 Frankfurt IAA where the company was ostensibly 'dipping its corporate toe in the waters', so to speak. Public reaction to the unusually styled TT coupé and roadster was positive and so in 1999 the Audi TT roadster and TT coupé arrived on Audi showroom floors across the world, where they were a sensation. Based on the Golf platform – *CAR* described them as a 'Golf in lingerie' – but with Audi-designed four-cylinder in-line dohc engines using the company's newly

Who would have thought that arch-conservative Vauxhall would build a sports car? The company has and it has been an image changer as well as popular with the sports car fraternity. (Photograph courtesy of Vauxhall)

Above *The TT was the mould breaker for the famous German company, it changed the way people saw Audi. Available with either front- or all-wheel drive, the TT roadster has enjoyed remarkable success. (Photograph courtesy of Audi AG)*

Below *The availability of a V6 engine option has revitalized sales and enthusiasm for the TT roadster, giving it strong performance to go with the svelte style. (Photograph courtesy of Audi AG)*

developed five-valve cylinder head technology and the option of the company's famous quattro all-wheel drive system, the TT's soon became the in car for young trendies to have.

The 1.8-litre engine was available in two stages of turbo-tune – 180bhp and 225bhp – which meant that it was never short of performance. The lesser-powered roadster would zip from 0 to 60mph in 8.2sec and run to a maximum of 137mph (220km/h), while the more powerful edition blasted to 60mph in 6.7sec and on to a maximum of 147mph (237km/h). Despite having 'only' four cylinders, albeit turbocharged ones, the Audi TT was not to be sneered at or put down when it came to the ability to cover ground quickly.

Late in 2002 Audi announced the facelifted TT at the Paris Salon. Included in the revised range was a new top model, the TT 3.2 V6, available in both coupé and roadster bodies. New, too, was Audi's stunning new *Dopplekupplungsgetriebe* (DSG for those who cannot get their tongues around the word that translates literally to 'double-clutch gearbox'), which was an integral part of the quattro driveline. Power from the 3.2-litre quad-cam V6, shared with the VW Golf R32 and the Audi A3 3.2 quattro, was a healthy 250bhp at 6,300rpm. Maximum speed was a governed 155mph (250km/h), while acceleration from 0 to 100km/h took just 6.6sec.

Mercedes-Benz and BMW

Porsche's two main rivals in Germany – Mercedes-Benz and BMW – were also on the case with entries of their own, both heavily reliant on existing corporate components. The Mercedes-Benz SLK was virtually a C-Class sedan underneath with a shiny svelte suit of clothes on top. Like all 'proper' Mercedes-Benz automobiles the

Mercedes-Benz, along with BMW, was quick to join the burgeoning roadster revolution and created the SLK using many C-Class components. It was not as involving to drive as the Porsche Boxster. (Photograph courtesy of DaimlerChrysler)

Looking at the Market

After six years Mercedes introduced the second-generation SLK with styling that mimicked the SLR McLaren at the front. The new V6 engine brought much-needed performance improvement. (Photograph courtesy of DaimlerChrysler)

SLK was conventional in its engineering insofar as its engine was front-mounted, disposed longitudinally driving the rear wheels through either a five-speed manual or five-speed Mercedes-Benz made automatic gearbox.

Built on a wheelbase reduced by 12.4in compared with its C-Class sibling, the SLK was available with two engine options. The base engine was a 2-litre four-cylinder fuel-injected engine – the same as in the equivalent C-Class sedan. Available as an option was the company's 2.3-litre dohc in-line four-cylinder *Kompressor* engine that developed 197bhp at 5,500rpm and 207lb ft of torque at 2,500rpm. Neither engine was a paragon of smoothness, nor possessing any particular verve.

The SLK's big-selling feature, however, was its electrically folding all-steel roof. At the press of a button – you had to be stationary, gear selector in Park, handbrake on – the roof would lift and fold in two places as it retracted into the luggage space behind the rear shelf. With the roof retracted there was room only for the proverbial G-string and toothbrush in the boot. That never seemed to be a sales stumbling block though.

Built in the former Borgward plant in Sebaldsbrück on the outskirts of Bremen in the north of Germany, the SLK has been a strong-selling sports car internationally for almost a decade now with only minor upgrades along the way. The most significant of those appeared for the 2000 model year. The base model became the SLK200 and was powered by a 161bhp Kompressor engine that boosted performance significantly. Top speed was 138mph (220km/h) and the 0–100km/h time was 8.2sec. Next up the line was the familiar SLK230 Kompressor that was a second quicker to 100km/h and 10mph faster at the top end. The company finally succumbed to pressure and offered the torquey but not especially powerful – 218bhp, 229lb ft – 3.2-litre sohc per bank eighteen-valve V6 engine as an option in an effort to match Porsche and BMW. Compared with the SLK230K that had a 0–60mph time of 7.2sec and a maximum speed of 148mph (238km/h), the SLK320 improved the acceleration by only 0.2sec and the top speed by a mere 3mph! For those wanting manic performance and who simply had to have an SLK, there was the 354bhp

Above Like Mercedes-Benz, the BMW entrant to the roadster market relied heavily on 'donated' sedan components, in this case the old 3 Series. Initially available with a weak four-cylinder engine, it nonetheless was a huge seller for the company. (Photograph courtesy of BMW GB)

Below New for 2002 was the completely re-engineered and styled Z4 with its controversial 'flame surfacing' side panels. It now featured the superior Z-axle rear suspension and was a far more involving sports car than the Z3. (Photograph courtesy of BMW GB)

SLK32 AMG that blasted to 60mph from rest in 5.2sec and had an electronically governed top speed of 155mph (250km/h).

New for 2004 was a completely restyled SLK that borrowed many cues from the sensational Mercedes-McLaren SLR. It is both more attractive and more powerful (and more costly!) with three new engines on offer: a 163bhp supercharged 2-litre in the SLK 200 Kompressor; 272bhp from a completely new quad-cam 3.5-litre V6 in the SLK 350; and an enormous 360bhp from a Mercedes-AMG V8 in the SLK 55 AMG. Performance varies from quick to electrifying, the AMG version rocketing from 0–100km/h in a mere 4.9sec, although maximum speed is still electronically limited to 155mph (250km/h).

Before BMW released the Z3, it had whetted the market's appetite with the unusually designed and now very collectible Z1, a product from its 'think tank', BMW Technik GmbH, which is located close to the main factory and head office in München. A roadster like the Z3, Z1 featured a steel chassis clothed with specially configured plastic outer panels, its pièce de résistance being the drop-down doors. In many ways the Z1 was something of a production experiment from which BMW learned many valuable lessons

Whilst its front suspension was pure 3-Series, at the rear the engineers at BMW Technik had devised what they referred to as the Z-axle, owing to the shape of one of its components. It was a multi-link type of independent rear suspension that eliminated the huge variations in camber which were endemic in the semi-trailing arm design that BMW had persisted with since 1961. When expert road testers drove the Z1 they were astonished at the levels of roadholding and the way in which the handling of the car was transformed by the new rear suspension system. Little did people realize that in the next 3-Series the same suspension system would appear and similarly transform BMW's best-selling range of models.

Like the SLK, the BMW Z3 was a cocktail of parts already available off the shelf. The Z3's chassis was a throwback in many ways to the discontinued E23 3-Series. Rather than use the new E36 Series' chassis and running gear, the Z3 picked up the outmoded old semi-trailing arm independent rear suspension, not the vastly superior Z-axle. It was clearly a decision based on costs. And the media hounded BMW on that point for the life of the model – it must have seemed like a good idea to the Board at the time, but such parsimony rather backfired on BMW.

From a design perspective, the BMW Z3 was an unusual amalgam of styling ideas and cues. The front was strong, even aggressive, but the rear was weak and looked incomplete, while the clamshell! bonnet (something that BMW was noted for with its Neue Klasse and original 02 models) with its broad *nieren* was pure BMW.

A rather anaemic 1.9-litre sohc in-line four-cylinder engine of just 118bhp at 5,500rpm and 133lb ft of torque at 3,900rpm powered the first Z3's that rolled off the company's brand new production lines at Spartanburg in South Carolina, USA. Performance was not particularly quick – brisk is probably the kindest way of describing it – 0–60mph took 10.4sec and its maximum speed was 122mph (196km/h). But that did not hinder sales, which took off like a rocket to the point where BMW was embarrassed for supplies in many markets outside America and Germany.

Gradually supplies caught up with demand that was stimulated by the addition of the excellent 192bhp 2.8 litre dohc in-line six-cylinder engine, also inherited from the 3-Series. With this power plant, performance was exhilarating – 0–60mph in 6.7sec and maximum speed rose to 134mph (216km/h).

A mid-model reshuffle of specifications saw the addition of a 2.2-litre version of the company's famous six-cylinder engine appear under the hood at one end of the spectrum, and the 2.8-litre six was replaced by the 3.0-litre six at the other. The 2.2 produced 170bhp at 6,100rpm and 125lb ft of torque at 3,500rpm and pushed the Z3 to 60mph in 7.9sec and a maximum speed of 139mph (224km/h). The 3.0-litre pumped out a healthy 231bhp and 221lb ft of torque to make a quick car even quicker – 0–60mph in 6.0sec and a maximum speed of 149mph (240km/h).

And just to keep its rivals honest, BMW raised the ante even further with the addition of the fabulous M GmbH 3.2-litre six-cylinder powerhouse from the M3 coupé under the Z3's shapely bonnet. Power output was an astonishing 325bhp at a manic 7,400rpm and its acceleration was a mind-numbing 5.4sec for the classic 0–60mph sprint. Top speed was electronically limited to 155mph (250km/h) under a gentleman's agreement between the German manufacturers. Only Porsche was not a co-signatory to the agreement.

In late 2002 BMW announced the Z4 to replace the now ageing Z3. In keeping with current BMW thinking, its Chris Bangle-inspired styling was full of 'flame' surfaces and odd shut lines but it was a very distinctive-looking roadster, one you were unlikely to lose in a crowd and one whose styling is unlikely to be mimicked. Its proportions were a carry-over from the Z3, that is, a long nose to house the six-cylinder engines (no four-cylinder engine is currently on offer or apparently likely in the short term, if ever, according to BMW GB) and a short, stumpy tail. Gone was the outmoded floorpan and under the Z4 was a chassis taken from the current E46 3-Series complete with the excellent Z-axle independent rear suspension.

According to *Autocar*, the Z4 can zip from rest to 100km/h in 5.9sec when powered by the 3-litre straight-six engine and is limited to 155mph as its maximum speed, making it fractionally quicker than the base 2.7-litre Boxster.

Nissan

Back in the early 1970s Nissan Motor Company surprised the world with the release of its 240Z sports coupé. While unique in body styling – reportedly credited to Graf von Goertz who also drew the legendary BMW 507 – its mechanical specification was a cocktail of corporate parts in exactly the same way as the BMW Z3 and Mercedes-Benz SLK. It seems it was less of an issue back then.

Its 2.4-litre sohc in-line six-cylinder engine produced 150bhp and endowed it with sparking performance for the era. Gradually the 240Z evolved into the 260Z and then the 280ZX before a total rethink saw the stylish 300ZX appear in late 1983 in Japan in naturally aspirated manual and automatic, manual-only turbocharged version and in two-seater and two plus two seater body configurations. Although it, too, used many off-the-shelf corporate parts nobody cared because the styling was absolutely stunning and the 3.0-litre 60-degree quad-cam V6 engine, especially in twin-turbocharged form that appeared in 1989 as part of a major model upgrade, offered superb performance. Magazines from the times quoted acceleration from rest to 60mph in 5.6sec and a maximum speed of 155mph. But it was a long, long way from the lithe and lean 240Z and Nissan found it increasingly difficult to sell, even in its main target market of America. Production was discontinued in 1994.

Time passed and in 1999 Nissan showed a 'teaser' concept model of a proposed Z car replacement that would rekindle the flame of the original 240Z. Certainly there were evocative styling cues which heightened that response from viewers and potential buyers. By late 2002 it was a production reality and Nissan announced to the world the arrival of the 350Z in coupé form with the promise of a convertible roadster to follow. True to Nis-

Looking at the Market

Following the success of the 350Z coupé, Nissan released the roadster soft-top version that has also been a huge success, especially in America. (Photograph courtesy of Nissan)

san's word, the car arrived in mid-2003. Power from the 3.5-litre 60-degree quad-cam V6 engine 276bhp is delivered to the rear wheels through a six-speed manual gearbox and gives the 350Z a maximum speed of 154mph (248km/h) and a 0–100km/h acceleration time of 5.9sec. Quick indeed.

The way in which Nissan went about teasing the market with a snappy-looking concept and then eventually producing a car of similar style and proportions was almost a carbon copy of the way in which Porsche prepared the market for its Boxster.

Looking at the Market

Sporty Smart

Recently, Germany's most innovative automobile manufacturer, Smart (which is based in Hambach, just over the Franco-German border near Saarbrücken) introduced the world to its latest creations, the roadster and roadster-coupé. Based on the platform and Tridion safety cell technology developed for the City coupé, these cars are powered by a 698cc sohc in-line triple-cylindered engine mounted transversely in the rear behind the two passengers' seats. The non-turbo engine delivers 61bhp at 5,250rpm while a more powerful turbo version produces 82bhp at the same 5,250rpm.

The Smart's performance is defined more by the cubic capacity of its engines than anything else. The lower-powered roadster runs to a maximum speed of 100mph (161km/h) exactly whilst its turbo sibling increases this to a fraction under 110mph (177km/h) according to factory figures. Fuel consumption, mind, is a frugal 4.9–5.0 litres per 62 miles (100km).

What is particularly appealing about the Smart roadster is its cheeky styling, something that was very deliberate. Inside is minimalist space and features for just two people; any overnight stay would involve minimal luggage.

Chrysler Crossfire and Mazda RX-8

In more recent times two further contenders have appeared on the market. First came the Chrysler Crossfire that is in reality a Mercedes-Benz SLK in V6 drag. It has a stunning exterior body design, is beautifully built by Karmann in Osnabrück, northern Germany, and has SLK-style refinement so it will be a sales success, particularly in America. The Mercedes-Benz-sourced 3.2-litre sohc V6 engine develops 218bhp at 5,700rpm and 229lb ft of torque at 3,000rpm – the same as in its Mercedes sibling. That makes it no slouch against the stop-

A cheeky interloper from the Smart division of the DaimlerChrysler company. It harks back to the days of the British Austin-Healey Sprite, MG Midget and Triumph Spitfire. It is light and nimble with a turbo-triple behind the two seats. (Photograph courtesy of Smart GmbH)

Chrysler has joined the fray with the new V6-engined Crossfire convertible. It is aimed mostly at the American market with some export appeal. (Photograph courtesy of DaimlerChrysler)

watch, taking 6.5sec to go from rest to 100km/h and it will run to a top speed of around 145mph (233km/h). A roadster version has been displayed and will become available shortly.

And then there is Mazda with its revolutionary Wankel-powered RX-8. Not only does it possess the charisma of the Wankel engine but also features a superbly styled body with, for the first time on a so-called sports coupé, four doors. The bugbear of all previous sports coupés was getting into the back seat. Mazda has neatly solved that one by designing the RX-8 with small rear-hinged ('suicide') doors. Like the Boxster, underneath the RX-8 is an engineer's delight with its multi-link wishbone suspension made from forged aluminium alloy components. Whether a genuine roadster version – the next generation RX-7 perhaps? – will appear is not yet clear.

Performance is pretty snappy, too, with the classic 0 to 100km/h acceleration time of 7.1sec and a top speed of 142mph (229km/h) from its 228bhp at 8,200rpm rotary engine. Its weakest point is its comparative lack of torque, 156lb ft at 5,500rpm from the 654cc twin-rotor Wankel.

Following the huge level of interest in the Boxster concept car in 1993, Porsche introduced the production version in late 1996 as a 1997 model year sports roadster. It has been a major success story for the company ever since.

And into this very crowded and very aware market came Porsche, the world's only exclusive large-scale manufacturer of sports cars. Its entry was by far the most charismatic and characterful, far more so than either the Mercedes or BMW. Unlike its two rivals' products, Porsche's new entry into the sports car market would be a bespoke Porsche through and through; it would not share any components with any mundane (if you can call a C-Class or a 3-Series mundane!) family sedan. No, the new Porsche Boxster would be pure unadulterated Porsche.

7 Boxster Meets the Press

Porsche released the Boxster at a gala event at the Schlosshotel Lerbach near the Odenwald (not far from Köln) between 23 August and 18 September 1996, where the world's media was given a full run-down on the new sports car's features as well as an extensive drive opportunity. This followed the Boxster's world unveiling at the 1996 Paris Salon, an event at which many remarked that it was the first all-new Porsche since the 928 of 1977 – very nearly two decades!

Porsche cars have always been favourites of the media and the expectation levels where the Boxster was concerned were sky high. From the first reports, there was some disappointment expressed as exemplified by Georg Kacher writing in *CAR* magazine, May 1996: 'It's not amazingly pretty, the Boxster, but it's certainly mould-breaking compared with its major rivals the BMW Z3 2.8 and Mercedes 230 SLK.'

Like many of his colleagues, Kacher lamented that fact that the production Boxster lost something in the translation from concept car to production car: 'It is not as intriguing as that stunning design exercise of 1993. The best bits haven't made it onto the production car, simply because they weren't practical.' He was referring to the front wings that were not large enough to accommodate two radiators; the side air intakes that were too small and too far away from the engine; the curved doors that were too short for easy entry and exit; the cute boot lid that limited luggage space and had no provision for the mandatory third brake light;

The presentation to the world's media took place at Schlosshotel Lerbach in suitably regal surroundings for what was a critical launch for Porsche.

Boxster Meets the Press

and there was nowhere to store the folding top.

However, Kacher did admit that the production car had some appealing features, from the fully integrated headlights–foglight–indicator units; ribbed air intake ahead of the rear wheels; chromed single central exhaust outlet; low drag mirrors; and flush-fitting door handles.

Pricing was always going to be a contentious issue with the media, although Porsche gave the appearance of being unconcerned about the matter. The Boxster came on to the UK market at £34,000, making it quite a bit more expensive than the comparable BMW Z3 2.8 and Mercedes-Benz SLK Kompressor. Various options available from the start – Tiptronic S automatic transmission, automatic air conditioning, hardtop, Sports suspension and wheels, various sound systems – all added considerably to the final investment.

Autocar's Peter Robinson was suitably impressed by the Boxster's dynamic abilities when he drove it at Weissach. He wrote in the September 1996 issue:

> Each run, faster than the preceding one, increased my admiration for the Porsche. Yet even as the extent of the Boxster's remarkable grip and brilliant chassis dynamics became ever more apparent, all this objective evaluation was being eclipsed by the overpowering joy of driving a car so utterly dedicated to the creation of driving heroes. Every corner an event, every drive, no matter how short, an affair to savour.

Robinson, with true Australian frankness, also said: 'The Boxster is pure, taut, sparkling with desirability. That should not come as a surprise, of course, because the Boxster is a bespoke sports car and not a roadster created from a donor sedan.' He was, as every reader knew,

Opposite *The Boxter's launch to the media at Schlosshotel Lerbach.*

Above *The new base model Boxster had a more powerful 2.7-litre flat-six engine and other enhancements.*

referring to the BMW Z3 and SLK Mercedes-Benz. Interestingly, Robinson was not critical of the production Boxster's styling because he recognized that the concept car, for all its beauty, was impractical and would never have passed the forthcoming crash safety test requirements.

On the subject of its performance he wrote: 'In terms of performance, the Boxster easily accounts for the Z3 and SLK [He must have been referring to the base model four-cylinder variants of each.], yet its appeal goes way beyond the claimed 6.7sec 0–60mph acceleration (7.4sec for the new five-speed Tiptronic with steering wheel button controls) and a 149mph top speed.' He also added in reference to the new wasserboxer engine, 'At 5,200rpm it delivers a passionate howl and hurls the car forward, changing to an even deeper wail at 6,000rpm. It's the sound of a fanatically eager engine, on its own justification for the £35,000 entry fee. Maybe it's never quite as quick as it feels, but that's no bad thing.'

Robinson, a vastly experienced motoring journalist who has been rarely wrong in his judgment of a car, was mightily impressed with the Boxster and said so.

Automobile, that most flamboyant of American motoring magazines, carried in its November 1996 issue driving impressions by Georg Kacher and a design analysis by the magazine's automotive design consultant Robert Cumberford. Despite the obvious and necessary changes forced on the design,

A suitably moody shot of a car – the Porsche Boxster S – which possesses dynamism and character that can be exploited at any time.

Cumberford summarized his critique by saying, 'We like it and are excited by the prospect of being able to drive an 'affordable' Porsche, but we still love the show car's outstanding panache.'

Joe Rusz, a well-known and respected Porschephile and then Senior Editor at *Road & Track*, that most European of American motoring magazines, wrote in reference to the Boxster's styling in the December 1996 issue:

> The Boxster show car sported such touches as low-mounted air intakes and roll hoops and generally looked like a vintage racing Porsche. At least until the platform and power train engineers got into the act. Faced with constraints of safety, packaging and practicality (not to mention cost), something had to give.

Getting away from it all – you and a Boxster S. Perfect! And what a great interior….

Happily, compromises made to satisfy real-world demands did not seriously deface Larson's dream which lost little in the translation.

Of its performance he said, 'A remarkably forgiving car for a mid-engined design, the Boxster carves up the slalom at 65mph, with mild understeer and extraordinarily precise turn-in. It's a reminder of why mid-engined sports cars are still made.'

Against the clock Rusz timed the Boxster at 6.1sec for the 0–60mph sprint, 14.7sec for the standing quarter mile and ran it to a maximum speed of 149mph (240km/h). It also took just 120ft (37m) to stop from 60mph, again a remarkable result.

Did Rusz find anything to criticize about the Boxster? Yes, he did, and it centred around the gearshift. He wrote: 'There's a bit of a gap between the gears in this modified Audi A6 gearbox. Okay, I'd pay extra for a six-speed. And for a proper shift linkage rather than the

cable shifter I sparred with, mostly on the 4–3 downshifts.' His colleague, Ron Sessions, also from *Road & Track*, drove another Boxster in convoy with Rusz and wrote in conclusion: 'Sports cars are the focus of Porsche and the grace and precision by which the Boxster moves, well, right out of the box, is testimony to that dedication. It's a natural.'

Autocar published a set of performance figures in its 5 February 1997 issue, having driven a Tiptronic-equipped car. Its figures were slightly down on those from *Road & Track*, achieving a 0–60mph time of 7.3sec and a maximum speed of 136mph (219km/h). It did comment, however, that the manual Boxster was faster and better.

Inevitably the Boxster was going to be compared with its German rivals. *What Car?* magazine carried a comparison test between the Boxster and the Mercedes-Benz SLK in its March 1997 issue. It was 2.3-litres four-cylinder supercharged versus 2.5-litre flat six-cylinder naturally aspirated; 193bhp versus 204bhp; 207lb ft of torque at 2,500rpm versus 181lb ft at 4,500rpm; five speed automatic (no manual was offered initially with the SLK) against a five-speed Tiptronic with the optional (£2,600!) steering wheel thumb buttons. Actual performance figures showed the Boxster had a significant edge over the SLK, recording 6.5sec for the 0–60mph sprint where the SLK took a comparatively slow 7.4sec; the passing acceleration for the vital 30–70mph (48–113km/h) range took 6.6sec for the Porsche, 7.7sec for the Mercedes, while their maximum speeds were near as dammit identical at 139mph (224km/h) for the Boxster and 140mph (225km/h) for the SLK. As the test drivers commented, 'The lower kerb weight makes the Porsche the faster car outright, and the more eager overtaker. Getting the best from it calls for harder work, though; its rev-hungry engine needs to spin above 4,500rpm to really come alive.'

In the driving dynamics *What Car?* found the two sports cars to be poles apart. The Boxster's roadholding was described as 'wonderfully tenacious', the steering and throttle 'super-responsive' and the brakes would 'hold back the tide'. The SLK was described as 'a completely different animal. A fast drive isn't as seductive an experience, but we've no qualms about the car's level of grip and safety.' It summarized: 'Even so, the Boxster out-performs it for pin-sharp steering, braking, handling responses and body control.'

In comparing the ride it thought the Boxster was firm without being objectionable, although the driver felt that the optional 17in wheels and low profile tyres were contributory factors to that minor criticism. He allowed that the SLK's ride was far more compliant, especially on A-roads and motorways. 'It's almost as accomplished a long-distance cruiser as a C-class saloon.' A rather poignant comment considering the car's bloodline.

Leaving aside depreciation factors and a £4,000 price advantage to the SLK, the *What Car?* crew summarized their feelings with two telling comments: 'The Mercedes can't match the Porsche's tingle factor;' and 'grab the keys to the Porsche, we say.'

Autocar, too, carried out a 'twin test' (3 September 1997, no. 4275) between the Boxster and the newly released BMW Z3 2.8, posing the question: 'Is the BMW Z3's great engine, keen pricing and enticing bundle of standard kit enough to rattle the purely hewn, mid-engined Porsche Boxster?'

Against the clock the Boxster was slightly quicker than the Z3 2.8, recording 6.5sec for the 0–60mph run versus 6.7sec; but in the standing start quarter-mile the tables were turned, the Z3 being timed at 15.2sec at 93mph (150km/h), while the Boxster took 15.6sec and 90mph (145km/h); passing acceleration for the critical 30–70mph bracket took 5.9sec for the Z3 and 6.6sec for the Boxster; and their maximum speeds were 134mph (216km/h) for the Z3 2.8 and 139mph

Porsche stylist Steve Murkett's sketch of a proposed sports car, one of many the stylists drew in the time leading up to the creation of the Boxster concept car and, ultimately, the production Boxster.

Following the successful showing of the Boxster concept car in Detroit, Porsche produced a 'competition' version, but it was only a teaser.

A clever longitudinally sectioned Boxster that shows everyone how tight the packaging was and how resourceful the Porsche engineers and designers were.

A superb technical cutaway drawing of the Boxster for those with a technical frame of mind and who enjoy seeing how the parts all fit together.

Right Like its 914 cousin, the Boxster boasts front and rear luggage compartments that allow owners to carry real cases on long journeys.

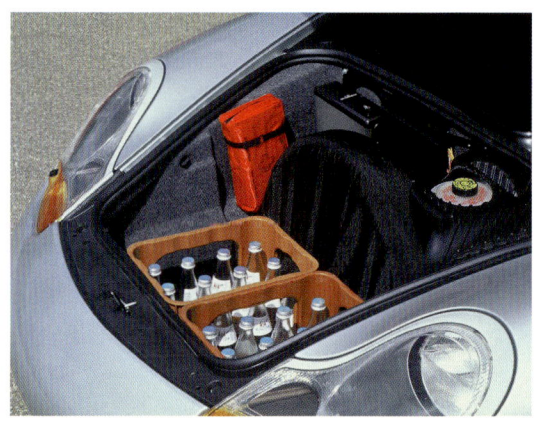

Below The ever creative people at Porsche have demonstrated here that the Boxster can to carry almost as much as a regular, but boring, saloon.

Above *For Boxster owners who want a more snug environment in inclement weather, Porsche has available a lightweight hardtop that seals the interior from the cold and damp outside.*

Below *The two Boxster models together. The exterior clues between them are subtle until you put them against the stopwatch, when the superiority of the S comes to the fore.*

RUF makes a small number of specialized Boxsters each year; these are Boxsters for a discerning clientele who enjoy the extra power and performance.

Above This is a rare photo of a hand-built Boxster prototype in Weissach.

Below Gemballa leads the pack in high horsepower Boxsters with its GTR500, the 500 referring to the engine's output. This machine is seriously quick; its 0–100km/h acceleration time is less than 4sec and it is capable of around 186mph (300 km/h)!

Above Not the most powerful Gemballa Boxster – that's the GTR500 – but still one of the most charismatic cars to drive is the torquey 3.9 edition from Uwe Gemballa.

Below The distinctive rear of the Gemballa Boxster.

Above Quite possibly the most beautiful mid-engined Porsche ever created. Not only was it beautiful, but it was a successful and versatile racer and is a car much-coveted by collectors today.

Below The Porsche Type 718 RS60 was a development of the 550 Spyder. Both cars greatly contributed towards the reputation of the company.

Above In the early post-war years the Porsche Bureau under the leadership of a young Ferry Porsche created the technically brilliant Cisitalia AWD racing car for the Italian Count Dusio.

Below Ferry Porsche at the wheel of the first Porsche – the 356–1. This particular example has been fully restored.

Above and Right For the 2003 model year Porsche offered a limited edition 550 Spyder version of the Boxster to commemorate the fifty years since the immortal Spyder was first available. Naturally it was an immediate sell-out!

The giveaway sign of the huge performance potential in the Boxster S – the four-pot bright red brake calipers.

(224km/h) for the Boxster. This was the Boxster's only clear-cut superiority over the Z3 2.8.

The test drivers summed up by writing: 'The Boxster's reputation is barely bruised by this scrap. It's the most complete and capable car Porsche makes and is far too good for the Z3 – even one with a smooth and brawny 2.8-litre straight six under the bonnet and a £6,000 price advantage in its favour.' They further commented:

> On the move, the gap grows alarmingly. Not only is the Boxster's body structure much stiffer than the Z3's, but its dynamic resolve is stronger, too. It turns in with more acuity, hangs on longer, rides bumps and ruts with more control and less shudder, and rakes as only a Porsche really can. It is both more focused and more complete.

Their final summation left no doubt about their feelings: 'In the end, it isn't so much what the Boxster does but the quality way in which it does it. This is a great Porsche.'

Douglas Kott from *Road & Track* wrote a detailed article in the November 1997 issue on a back-to-back drive of the Boxster versus the BMW Z3 2.8. He said, 'After years of specialization – BMW with its sports sedans, Porsche with its 2+2 sports and grand touring cars – these two German power houses, purveyors of enthusiast cars par excellence, were about to lunge at each other and lock horns in the 2-seat roadster segment.' Further into the article he discussed the merits and faults of the two protagonists, commenting on their ride/handling by saying of the Boxster, '...the Boxster is more adept at changing directions quickly, aided by steering that's quick though somewhat numb-feeling when held to the high standard of the '993' 911.' He also commented negatively about the Boxster's relatively poor cable gearshift linkage, and the amount of understeer at low speeds, but he loved the car's superb brakes – 'The brakes need no qualifying statement: stopping distances are ultra-short, and response is immediate.'

Where the BMW was concerned, Kott said, 'The BMW Z3 2.8 revels in being throttle-steered. Given a suitable skidpan or racetrack sweeper, you can practice your Tazio Nuvolari impressions all day long with tail-out lurid

At certain times of the year many owners want to block out the miserable weather and travel in warmth and comfort. The optional lightweight hardtop almost turns the Boxster into a coupé.

slides.' He felt that the Z3 was tidier than the Boxster in daily sports driving – 'the front and rear ends of the car worked in concert, but it should be noted that everything is happening at a less dizzying level of grip.' The BMW's gearshift was far more precise and its brakes were virtually a match for those of the Boxster. Although he did not nominate a winner, it was clear from his article that he preferred the Boxster.

Mark Gillies, writing in the American magazine *Automobile*, said of the Boxster, having awarded it the magazine's Car of the Year:

> Driving a great sports car should be natural. There shouldn't be surprises, just revelations. It should stimulate and enthral. It should be a two-way conversation between the driver and the car, with the driver talking, the car responding, and with the driver reacting.

That's just how it is with the Boxster because the controls are so well weighted and precise. Where some cars are let down by inert steering, spongy brake-pedal response, or clumsy turn-in, the Boxster is perfectly balanced and utterly communicative.

Curiously, *Autocar* published in their 'Why I Hate The…' column (it's on the last page of the magazine) in the 16 September 2003 issue a hate session by Andrew Frankel on the Porsche Boxster. He opened his commentary by saying, 'I guess what I hated about the Porsche Boxster was not so much the car as the concept. If the 911 was a triumph of evolution over engineering, so the original Boxster's victory was one of style over substance. And I dreaded what it would do for the marque.' As Frankel readily admitted, Porsche was in financial trouble and the company 'needed a car that would sell to people who'd buy chicken pox if it had a Porsche badge on it. The Boxster was the result and, no question, it saved the company. But that didn't mean that I had to like it.' He further added, 'In 2.5-litre form, the Boxster was not a driver's car; it was a poseur's car.' Pretty cynical stuff.

8 Improving Upon Perfection

From the moment it was released it was clear to the Porsche management that the 12,000 Boxsters a year that they had originally planned to build would never be sufficient to meet the burgeoning international demand. And so, working on the premise that if it ain't broke don't fix it, the engineers and stylists at Porsche have been having a relatively easy time at work lately. It has been more a case of fiddling with the details because buyers were clearly happy with the car.

In 1997, the Boxster's first full production year, Porsche did not offer its clients the option of 18in wheels. Many (mostly German) owners, therefore, went to their nearest Porsche performance specialist tuner who was only too keen to fit the larger wheels. Unbeknown to either the owners or the tuners this proved not to be a good idea as the rear structure of the body was not sufficiently rigid to take the added forces these wheels and tyres could generate. Therefore, for the 1998 model year the factory reinforced the rear part of the body with stronger suspension anchorage points, rear cross member, engine compartment bulkhead and wheel well strut mounts. An important point here is not to fit 18in wheels to any pre-MY98 Boxsters.

For 1999 the fuel tank was increased in capacity from 57 to 64 litres, the same capacity as the 911, and that resulted in an increase in the car's cruising range of up to 50 miles.

Very little had changed from the original – after all, if it ain't broke why fix it?

Improving Upon Perfection

Many thousands of hours were spent dyno-testing the forthcoming Boxster S before its release.

Stronger wheel hubs were specified, too.

Over and above the standard trim offered in the Boxster, buyers had for 1999 the offer of two packages that enabled the client to individualize the interior of his or her car. The Classic equipment package according to Porsche 'emphasizes a sophisticated but reserved style'. It included metallic paintwork and all-leather seats, and the windscreen frame and storage box covers in the doors and centre tunnel were finished in a granite-grey colour while the instrument surrounds, door closing handles and gearshift cover were finished in an amber colour. And then there was the Trend interior trim package that used Graffiti Grey in conjunction with panels finished in the car's body colour. It was available only in Zenith Blue metallic and Dragonfly Turquoise metallic paintwork. The roof was Graffiti Grey and the seats were finished in Graffiti Grey/Charcoal Grey, while the steering wheel, handbrake lever, door handles and gearshift lever knob were all in black leather. The instrument panel, interior door lining, centre console cover, instrument and airbag covers were also finished in Graffiti Grey, while the instrument surrounds, A-pillar, door surrounds, rollbars and the insert on the gear lever knob were all painted in the car's body colour.

Many items that were previously combined in the sports package were now available as individual items if that's the way a buyer wanted to order his or her Boxster. For example, the

With the increased performance of the 3.2 S, Porsche had to ensure that airflow management around the Boxster S was perfect.

sports seats with enhanced side bolsters, or the sports suspension with the firmer springs, harder dampers and thicker stabilizer bars; or the newly available 18in turbo-look alloy wheels that were fitted with 225/40 ZR front and 265/35 ZR rear tyres that were, incidentally, the same size as those fitted on the high performance 911 Carrera.

New for 1999 was the availability of Litronic headlights, special gas discharge lights that illuminated the road far more brightly for improved night driving safety. Not only were the headlight's beams stabilized, but also when the driver activated high beam the Litronic low-beam lights remained on and raised their beam ever so slightly to improve further the illumination of the road ahead – Porsche called it 'dynamic headlight range control'. Headlight washers came with the option.

Apart from the few who mourned the loss of the panache of the Boxster concept car – they seemed to miss the intention of the words 'concept car' – the only real complaint that was levelled at the sports car was its comparative lack of get up and go. The 2.5-litre engine, while smooth, reasonably punchy and aurally delightful, lacked the outright urge that Porsche drivers seemed to demand.

Rumour Made Real – The Boxster S

And so Porsche called the world's media to Colli del Tronto in Italy in July 1999 to show them that the company was listening and had reacted to the complaint. Porsche introduced the long-awaited new range that included the eagerly anticipated and much rumoured Boxster S.

Improving upon what was perceived by many to have been near-perfection was always going to be a difficult task for the Porsche stylists and engineers. There was no way that they

The 2000 model year cars, which included the new Boxster S, were shown to the media in the Italian Alps – a wonderful setting for a wonderful sports car.

It looks glorious, sounds great. Pity the photo cannot describe the sound!

were going to alter the finely-honed lines of the original, so it had to be in the details that any change would, or could, take place. It would be another extremely discreet makeover.

The Boxster S featured a new moulded front bumper/spoiler now with a third air inlet in the centre to allow cooling air over the third radiator, the assembly giving the S a slightly more masculine appearance. At the rear, the S now had dual exhaust outlets and on the engine hood the letter 'S' was added to the name Boxster, both being Titanium coloured, as was a garnish trim around the front windscreen and the grille bars in the bumper (they had previously been black). Other exterior enhancements for the Boxster S included the fitting of stronger 17in alloy wheels as standard – 18in alloys were optional – and the brake calipers were now painted red with the Porsche name embossed upon them.

Inside, discreet chrome plating was applied to the door handles and pulls, gearshift inlay and handbrake release. The seats were upholstered in a high-quality Alcantara material (not available on the S in the UK) and there was a new cloth inner hood lining. An alarm system was fitted that provided full surveillance of the

Improving Upon Perfection

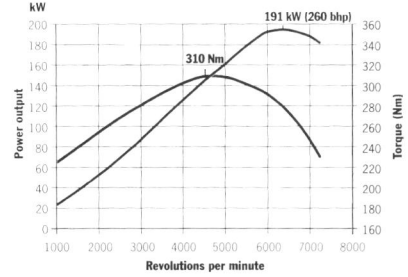

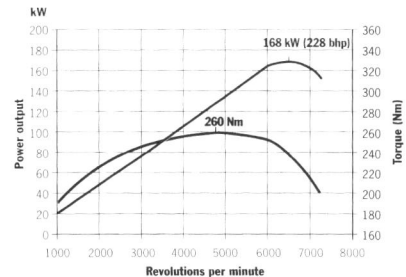

It looked very little different from the original 2.5 but it added measurably to the Porsche driving experience. Bosch DME 7.2 electronics assisted in a smooth power delivery as well as superior fuel economy (if that was important!). The graphs above right demonstrate the power output.

interior – already available in the UK – with an infra-red remote opener was standard, as was a sporting three-spoke leather-rimmed steering wheel. There were now greyish-silver faced instrument dials and aluminium-coloured surrounds encompassing the instruments as well as discreet 'Boxster S' motifs on each doorsill.

Some critics said that the update was little more than window dressing. Be that as it may, the model year upgrades are going to provide considerable fodder for Boxster-spotting anoraks in years to come, as they are so sublime in the way in which they have been applied.

For the Boxster S, increasing the cylinder bore diameter to 93mm increased the engine's capacity to 3,179cc. Larger valves – 37.1mm for the inlet and 32.5mm for the exhausts – helped power to rise to 252bhp at 6,250rpm and torque to 225lb ft at 4,500rpm. Incidentally, those valve sizes were identical to those in the 911 Carrera. The engine's redline was 7,200rpm assisted by a new two-stage resonance intake manifold.

Porsche claimed the new Boxster S with the six-speed manual gearbox would accelerate from rest to 100km/h in just 5.9sec and would reach a maximum speed of 161mph (260km/h).

New, too, was the adoption of Bosch's latest DME 7.2 electronic engine management system that had proven itself in the Carrera 4, which also saw the demise of the traditional cable-operated accelerator linkage, to be replaced by the 'drive by wire' system. Porsche dubbed it the E-gas system and touted its advantages to include better and smoother control of load change reactions, and to give greater harmony when starting off, when changing gears in the Tiptronic S transmission and in the anti-spin control mode.

E-gas was now being fitted as standard equipment to the 911 Carrera and the two Boxster models. It seemed such a trivial thing

103

Improving Upon Perfection

With the arrival of the Boxster S the five-speed Tiptronic automatic gearbox was now shared with the 911.

– doesn't everybody have it? – that little was made of it at the time. Basically it consisted of a throttle unit driven by an electric motor that was controlled by the Motronic 7.2 computer.

Two trimetal-coated three-way catalytic converters were incorporated in the Boxster S's twin-chamber exhaust system and by operating in conjunction with an air-injection system they enable the car to comply with the Low Emission Vehicle (LEV) standards in America and the D4 requirements in Germany. A side issue of

---

E-Gas System

A feature that has proven its value in the Porsche 911 Carrera 4 is now being introduced in all variants of the 911 and the two Boxsters: Motronic ME 7.2 engine management with E-gas (electronic gas pedal).

E-gas replaces the conventional mechanical gas cable with a throttle unit driven by an electric motor and masterminded by the electronic 'brain' of the ME 7.2 Motronic. The throttle butterfly is adjusted by an electric motor connected via a two-stage transmission to the throttle butterfly shaft, thus ensuring electronic management and control of the air drawn in by the engine over the entire load range. The fine-tuning provided in this way is also used to dampen the load change response, at the same time serving to harmonize the process of setting off, shifting gears in the Tiptronic S transmission, and controlling wheel spin.

To obtain the feed signal controlling the butterfly, the gas pedal is connected by a short cable with a pedal position sensor converting gas pedal travel into an electrical signal transmitted to the control unit, which in turn sets the position of the throttle butterfly via an electric motor. The control unit also serves to adjust the ignition timing, speeding up the process of heating the catalytic converter by switching over to ignition retard and thus helping to minimize harmful emissions in the warm-up phase. The reduction in torque suffered in such a case is again set off by E-gas helping to enhance motoring comfort by gas pedal travel independent of engine temperature.

Two computers monitoring each other control system security and reliability. Two sensors each serve furthermore to report the position of the throttle butterfly and pedal sensor. The signals obtained are checked for feasibility by a direct comparison with the air mass meter, and fail-safe functions are activated in the event of a deficiency, ensuring that the driver is able to reach the next workshop.

Improving Upon Perfection

Lower Emissions: Fit for LEV and D4

As an automobile manufacturer Porsche has taken its responsibilities for reduced exhaust emissions very seriously. And as Germany's premier manufacturer of sports cars it is doubly important because its clients expect that there will be no reduction in the driving pleasure associated with owning a Porsche.

Porsche has been pursuing a specific policy in emission management for many years using a metal substrate in the three-way catalytic converters. This path is different from that taken thus far by most other manufacturers, who have been working with a ceramic substrate. A metal substrate is able to cope easily with the high temperatures involved and, contrary to the ceramic unit, efficiently dissipates so-called 'hot spots'. The new coating used for the first time on the model year 2000 Porsches was a combination of platinum, rhodium and palladium that ensured even better temperature resistance and it cut in at a lower temperature than the bi-metal coating used previously.

Another key issue in the emission management and conversion process is the subdivision of the metal substrate into two sections with the actual physical size of the catalyst remaining unchanged. Between the two metal sections is a swirl unit that makes the exhaust gas flow in a different direction. The remarkable result of this concept is that tiny particles of harmful emissions so far able to flow through the catalytic converter without touching the precious metal sections able to initiate the conversion process are now converted with a much higher level of efficiency. The swirl unit moves them out of their position and makes them hit the wall of precious metal in the second substrate section.

Operating in conjunction with secondary air injection, a technology carried over from the existing models, this new catalyst technology guarantees optimum efficiency. All versions of the 911 Carrera and both Boxsters comply with the strictest emission standards in the world. They outperform the extremely severe US LEV (Low Emission Vehicle) standard with limits reduced to 3.4 grams of Carbon Monoxide (CO) and 0.2 grams of Nitrous Oxide (NOX) per mile. They also comply with the German D4 standard and are eligible for a lower level of road tax in that country, with limits of 0.7 grams/km of CO, 0.08 grams/km of hydrocarbons, and 0.07 grams/km of nitrous oxides.

---

this technology was a lower road tax cost for Boxster S owners!

With this respecification of the range came cross-drilled brake discs (S only), and a six-speed close-ratio manual gearbox for the Boxster S, the gearshift pattern being the double-H type with reverse off to the left next to first gear. The standard model retained the original's five-speed unit; the Tiptronic S automatic remained at five speeds although it was now common with the more powerful 996 edition of the 911, and for drivers of the Boxster S so equipped there was a toggle switch on the steering wheel that allowed the driver to shift gears up or down even though the selector might be in the automatic position.

There were small but significant tweaks to the Boxster S's suspension settings, the springs and anti-roll bars being slightly firmer and the dampers quite a deal firmer. At the rear, there were revised wheel mounts and suspension bushes, together with a longer control arm that improved the toe-in stiffness during hard cornering. There were also larger wheel bearings.

Confirmation as the Boxster blasts past you that it was an S – the dual exhaust outlets.

Improving Upon Perfection

Ventilated and cross-drilled, the four-piston callipers of the Boxster S brakes provided safe and sure stopping at all times.

It's like a peep show: the bright red calipers peeking out from behind the spokes of the alloy wheels.

All of this higher performance capability of the Boxster S required a corresponding increase in braking performance. The front brake disc rotors, now cross-drilled for superior cooling, were increased in diameter to 318mm and the width to 28mm, while those at the rear were now 299mm in diameter and 24mm wide. New to the S was an aluminium-bodied four-piston monobloc caliper that had been patented by Porsche.

The Boxster S helped in marketing terms to bridge the gap between the Boxster and the new 911 that was powered by a 3.4-litre – soon to be increased to 3.6-litre – version of the company's new water-cooled boxer six-cylinder engine.

In all of the hoopla surrounding the S it could have been possible to overlook what Porsche refers to as the 'basic' Boxster. It, too, received an engine massage but not to the same extent as its sibling. The base engine was now out to 2,687cc in capacity through a longer crankshaft stroke of 78mm, the cylinder bore remaining at 85mm. Maximum power rose to 220bhp at 6,400rpm and torque was now 192lb ft at 4,750rpm. Included in the engine specifications was the new Motronic 7.2 management with the E-gas accelerator control and new catalytic converters that also allowed the 2.7-litre engine to qualify for USA LEV ratings as well as the German D4.

The gearbox ratios of the five-speed unit were altered slightly to cater for the increased power and torque of the engine. The 'basic' Boxster was, however, no sluggard and was capable of 155mph (250km/h) with acceleration from rest to 100km/h coming up in 6.6sec in the five-speed manual version. With the Tiptronic S, maximum speed was down slightly to 152mph (245km/h).

Improving Upon Perfection

Ventilated but not cross-drilled, the brakes of the basic Boxster were still very much up to the car's performance.

> **POSIP: Sidebags Standard**
>
> From the 2000 model year Porsche fitted its POSIP side airbag system as standard across its entire range of sports cars. POSIP is an acronym for Porsche Side Impact Protection and comprises side airbags offering the driver and passenger a broader scope of protection than that afforded by conventional side airbags. The side airbags offered by Porsche are equally as effective in both the coupés and open roadsters.
>
> Housed in the door panel, the airbag modules differ from conventional units also through their large volume and their geometry. In a side collision this ensures not only the usual protection for the occupant's chest and head, but also prevents the driver's and passenger's heads from hitting any side object.
>
> The side airbags are inflated when required by a hybrid gas generator. This minimizes the need for a complex pyrotechnical system. At the critical moment, argon and helium flow into the gas-tight airbags, triggered by a sensor on the doorsill and another on the instrument panel.

For future Boxster-spotting anoraks, the clues to look for inside include a new shift lever, new door openers, remote openers for the luggage compartments, side airbag symbols and a handbrake button in an aluminium look finish and, if the Boxster is fitted with the Tiptronic S option, the release button and selector lever gaiter also have an aluminium look. And the front and rear lid release mechanisms have been changed to remote/electrical operation in place of the previously used cables.

Writing in the Australian magazine *Wheels*, Peter Robinson said, 'Porsche's Boxster S was on stand-by for 12 months waiting for a call from marketing. The regular Boxster was so much in demand that Zuffenhausen deemed it foolish to launch a more powerful, more expensive version of its mid-engined roadster. Finally, the call has come.' He went on to say, 'that the S should be midway between the Boxster and Carrera in performance; that it should be interesting enough to attract current Boxster owners, but not so fast that it cannibalizes 911 sales.' He concluded by saying, 'More than anything, the S proves Porsche knows how to make an improved car. The problem now facing the marketing people is how to justify the existence of the Carrera Cabriolet when the Boxster S is almost as quick, more fun to drive and considerably cheaper.'

MOTOR, the more extrovert of the two mainstream Australian motoring magazines, compared the Boxster S with the BMW M roadster. The BMW was marginally quicker in acceleration and more hoonish to drive near the limit, but the article concluded that the clinical ability of the Boxster slightly outweighed that of the BMW, and so by the narrowest of margins went for the Boxster S.

Is that a glorious sight or what? Beautiful car with the mountain valley behind filled with early morning cloud. Bellissima!

Model Year 2001

For the 2001 model year a number of specification upgrades took place. The Boxster received the same soft-top hood as the S insofar as it, too, now featured the cloth headliner which reduced noise levels significantly. Further, there was now soft-touch material on the integrated safety bars and the three-spoke steering wheel had the coloured Porsche crest proudly displayed on its hub. Better quality carpets were fitted in the luggage compartments; there was now an LED lighting for the interior, console, ignition lock and door handles; the spoiler light went off after the engine was started and there was a new light to let you know if one or both of the trunks was open; the electric windows now went back up once the top latch had been closed and they had an auto-retraction system if they sensed an obstruction (like an arm or a finger); and the fuel filler cap now had a rubberized 'chain' on it to prevent it from being lost. And the digital speed read-out was moved from the tachometer to the speedometer, a far more sensible positioning.

Model Year 2002

Porsche Stability Management (PSM) was now an option for both Boxsters, as was a new sub-woofer speaker system. The sound system option was made even more attractive for MY02 with the offering of a BOSE system in place of the previous digital system; there was a new multi-function display in the lower segment of the tachometer when the optional on-board computer was ordered. New seat

Improving Upon Perfection

Six years young but still with what it takes to pull the crowd. Few sports cars can boast that!

Porsche Stability Management (PSM)

When ordering your Boxster you can tick the box marked PSM and enjoy the benefits of an all-encompassing electronic system that will watch over your every driving moment. It sounds a little Big Brotherish, but it's not meant to be that way – you can deactivate it by simply pressing a console-mounted button. But what exactly is PSM?

PSM is an active control system for stabilizing a car – in this case a Boxster – at the limit of its driving dynamics capability. PSM includes such functions as ABS (anti-block system), ABD (automatic braking differential), ASR (traction-slip control), EBV (electronic brake force distribution), as well as a longitudinal dynamics control system MSR (engine drag torque control). In addition, the vehicle is stabilized at the limit of its driving dynamics capability within the transverse dynamics control system by FDR (driving dynamics control system).

The system will allow the best possible traction during acceleration and braking no matter what the coefficient of friction of the road surface is; it will prevent dynamic oversteer during sudden changes of direction or when the driver lifts off the power mid-corner; it will reduce understeer when entering a corner too quickly; it will provide shorter braking distances and stability particularly where the road surface is inconsistent; it can compensate for load-reversal reactions when accelerating or braking in a corner up to the maximum latitudinal acceleration on all road surfaces.

The system can be deactivated and in this mode only the ABS and ABD functions remain active.

Interestingly, Porsche offers a caveat in its service information book on PSM. It reads, 'PSM preserves driving stability and considerably increases driving safety. However, not even PSM is capable of cancelling out the limits of automobile physics! With PSM the driver is still totally responsible for his driving actions.'

Improving Upon Perfection

A desirable sports car at rest, a rare sight.

belts with pretensioners and force limiters were fitted as standard.

Model Year 2003

Now six years in the market place and a huge sales success for the company, Porsche announced after the August holidays in 2002 (for the 2003 model year) again slightly modified Boxsters. And again it was the little details that came in for scrutiny. For the top model, the Boxster S, there was a modicum more power, with the engine now being rated at 260bhp at 6,200rpm with torque also increasing slightly to 421lb ft at 4,600rpm. These gains boosted the performance ever so slightly; the classic 0–100km/h sprint taking 5.7sec and the maximum speed was now quoted as 164mph (264km/h). Despite this added power and performance, Porsche claimed 2 per cent greater fuel economy – a bit like having your cake and eating it too! This was all possible through the agency of Porsche's VarioCam Plus technology that could adjust the cam timing infinitely up to an angle of 40 dgerees, which, as an added benefit, reduced charge cycle losses in the process. To cope with this extra brio, both the gears and the clutch were strengthened, the clutch now exerting a higher contact pressure. Gearbox ratios for both the six-speed manual and five-speed Tiptronic S,

It may seem strange to many, but the arrival of a lockable glovebox (which also featured a light) was a big deal for Boxster owners.

VarioCam Plus

Two Engine Concepts in One

From the 2002 Model Year Porsche offered VarioCam Plus on all models throughout its range, this being a technological step forwards from the VarioCam system that had been in use on Porsche engines since the 944 days. Camshaft adjustment on the intake side (Vario-Cam) was now supplemented by a valve lift control that also operated on the intake side (Plus). Featured originally on the 911 Turbo, the new system was able to optimize engine output and performance on the one hand, while, on the other, reducing fuel consumption and exhaust emissions, and improving running smoothness and refinement.

The valve adjustment system is made up of switching cup tappets on the intake side of the engine, operated by an electro-hydraulic switching valve. With two different cam contours on the intake camshaft, the engine always runs on the appropriate lift curve with the cams switching from one to the other. The cup tappets are made up of two interacting elements locked against the other with the assistance of a bolt. This creates a direct link, first between the inner tappet and the small cam and, second, between the outer tappet and the large cam. A hydraulic compensation unit for valve play is integrated in all cases in the tappet's force flow line.

Variable Valve Lift

VarioCam Plus really means two engine concepts in one. As long as the engine is idling, valve lift is controlled by the small cams to a maximum limit of 3.6mm, and valve timing is optimized to keep any valve overlap to a minimum. The small valve lift reduces friction, significantly increases the charge motion thanks to the very short opening times, and reduces emissions from any previous combustion within the combustion chambers. A further advantage is the reduction in fuel consumption (by up to 10 per cent), together with a much more smooth and stable idle.

Under part load the engine should run with internal recirculation of exhaust gases in order to minimize any throttle effect and again to reduce fuel consumption. To achieve this, valve lift is shifted to a large overlap area that is a long period for drawing in exhaust gases. Under full load, superior torque and engine output are ensured by a highly efficient gas charge cycle with minimum losses, on the one hand, and an uncompromising cam contour on the other that has 11mm maximum valve lift with suitably adjusted opening and closing times during the valve cycle.

VarioCam Plus also helps, before you begin, by considerably improving the engine's starting characteristics when cool and by reducing emissions when the engine is warming up.

Both of the VarioCam Plus systems – camshaft adjustment and valve lift control – are masterminded by the Motronic ME7.8 with its high standard of operating and vast computing capacity that has been designed especially for these particular requirements. This is important since that factors required for controlling VarioCam Plus are, in particular, engine speed, accelerator position, engine oil and coolant temperature, as well as recognition of the gear currently in use. The driver's commands in terms of engine power or torque are compared with control maps within the system, the Motronic unit, then deciding within milliseconds how VarioCam Plus should respond.

however, remained unchanged.

There were also new ten-spoke 17in light-alloy road wheels as standard and five-spoke 18in alloys that had originally been seen on the 911 Carrera. Both were lighter than previous wheels, the 17in by 4.4lb (2kg) a set and the 18in by a remarkable 2.8lb (10.8kg).

And the folding soft-top convertible roof was redesigned to incorporate a fourth roof bracket that was positioned above the rear window that was now made from glass. Naturally, electric heating elements for demisting were a standard fitting, although they were slightly smaller than before.

To say that the changes in design were discreet would be something of an understatement. The Boxster's design has been universally acclaimed after a perhaps begrudging reception from the world's media, but even they have grown to admire what Porsche has achieved. For the 2003 model year there was a newly designed front bumper with a

Improving Upon Perfection

The vent strakes were brought forward to be almost flush with the outer rim for MY03.

As a part of the rejuvenation of the Boxster range for MY03, the centre console was a modified 911 unit.

For improved aerodynamics, Porsche enlarged the rear spoiler for 2003.

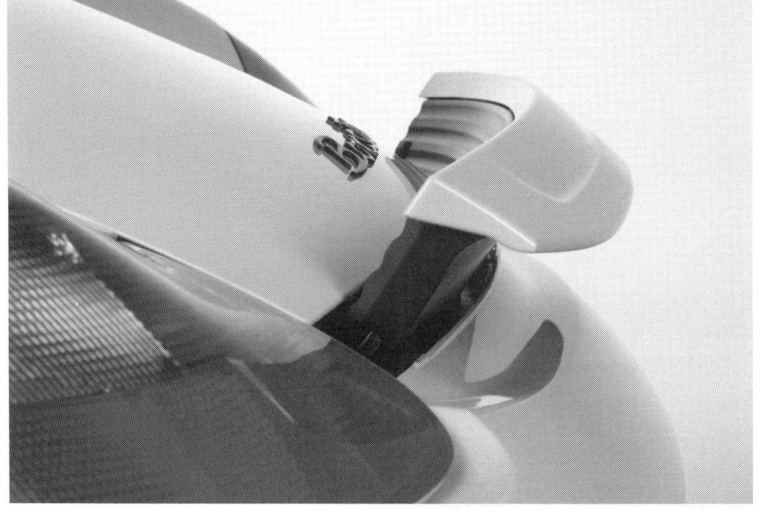

pronounced lower lip (aerodynamic advantages were claimed) and a revised design for the air scoops on either side at the front that were now curved further around the outside to give what Porsche described as 'a more elegant and dynamic look [that] gives the entire front end of the car a more pronounced and distinctive arrow shape.' There were apparent aerodynamic advantages and an improved flow of cooling air to the front-mounted radiators. The Boxster S retained its characteristic third, central, air intake and the grilles were now painted the body colour.

The side vent grilles, too, were now painted the body colour, the horizontal grille bars being brought forward in the opening and the grille itself was now a one-piece plastic moulding where previously it was two assemblies.

A clear finish lens for the front, side and rear indicators arrived for 2003. At the rear (of the S) were newly styled twin exhaust tailpipes and two distinctive crossbars in the lower bumper valance. Again, aerodynamic testing showed the new arrangement to have benefits for air management at the rear as well as better extraction of air heated by the exhaust

Another change welcomed by Boxster owners and enthusiasts was the change to a glass rear window with embedded electric demisting wires.

silencer. The new soft-top's shape, too, was modified for a better aerodynamic performance (it closely resembles the optional hard-top in silhouette now) and this in turn improved the airflow over the rear spoiler at speeds above 75mph (120km/h). The spoiler

---

New PCM Operating at the Speed of Light

A new technology with the name MOST (Media-Oriented Systems Transport) for exchanging multi-media data was made available as an option as of the 2003 model year Porsches.

The advantage of this system is that it uses lightwave conductors to exchange data between the various units without any loss of quality and it does so at very high speed. All functions of the radio, CD changer and amplifier units and the telephone are masterminded through the MOST lightwave conductors. When ordering the car, the client can specify the level of equipment and which are to be integrated into the system. By networking the Porsche Communication Management (PCM) with the instrument cluster via the Controller Area Network (CAN) the driver can display the current radio programme, music titles, incoming telephone calls and navigation pictograms on the screen.

PCM: A New Highlight

From the 2003 model year, the PCM has several new features to make it more user-friendly. It features a double-tuner, a CD player, dynamic route navigation, trip computer and a GSM dual-band telephone, all displayed on a new 5.8in colour screen. There is also a twelve-digit keyboard for entering telephone numbers or the frequency of a favourite radio station. A small insert below the keyboard accommodates the user's SIM card, dispensing with the need for an adaptor when using a mobile phone.

The front spoiler shape was altered slightly with a more pronounced lip around the lower edge for better air management.

itself was new – it was wider with a slightly raised profile incorporated into it and was 'more aesthetically pleasing', according to Porsche people. Owners found it easier to scratch when removing articles from the rear boot, however.

A further upgrade in standard fittings for the Boxster S saw a dual cupholder incorporated in the dash – you got the impression that Porsche was not happy to fit a cupholder as they saw it as a distraction from the real purpose of their sports car, that is, the driving experience. The remote car opener now had the facility to open not only the car itself but also the front and rear boot lids separately; and as on the 911 there was now a glove compartment with a light and the lock was linked to the car's alarm system. The BOSE sound system with CD stacker utilized the MOST optical-fibre bus for greater clarity of sound.

For the 'basic' Boxster there was a corresponding slight power increase, to 228bhp at 6,300rpm and to 192lb ft of torque at 4,700rpm. The 0–100km/h acceleration time was now quoted at 6.4sec and maximum speed as 157mph (253km/h). And there was a 2 per cent improvement in fuel economy, too. As with its S sibling, these performance gains were a direct result of improvements to the VarioCam Plus system. And as with its S sibling, the basic Boxster also featured a cupholder in the centre of the dash and the illuminated glovebox with a lock that was linked to the optional alarm system.

Porsche flew the media to Italy for the 2003 model year upgrade where they were greeted

Improving Upon Perfection

by a substantially unchanged sports car!

What did the media have to say about the latest titillations to the Boxster? Chris Horton, editor of *911 & Porsche World* magazine, made several comments in the August 2002 issue. Among them was a reference to the Boxster's age, about which he wrote:

> The somewhat unpalatable truth, though, is that six years is a very long time in the car industry. And although the original Boxster might have looked relatively fresh, to continue producing it in more or less the same form in which it first appeared – and with increasing competition from the likes of Honda, Lexus, BMW and even possibly MG – really would have been an unacceptable risky strategy on Porsche's part.

He went on to say that, 'the latest cars clearly embody the German motor industry's long-established tradition of evolution rather than revolution.'

Telling the differences between old and new Boxsters was going to be a potential problem for buyers of used editions. Horton further commented:

> Certainly the Boxster has been around for quite a long time now, and apart from that much-publicized (and long overdue) hike in engine size and power in the autumn of 1999, it has received little, if anything, in the way of substantive updates. And it's equally true to say that despite still-impressive sales figures the innovative roadster was just – but only just – beginning to lose its must-have appeal.

Mike Duff, writing in *CAR*, August 2002, said:

> The best news about all these Boxster revisions is that they're free. Granted, you'll still need to find something over £30,000 for the actual Boxster. But all of the running mid-life mods haven't added to the asking price at all. And, within its very limited remit, the facelift has worked.

The rear bumper, too, was changed with a more pronounced edge and minor changes around the exhaust pipes and lower valance.

Improving Upon Perfection

You can see the beauty in motion; there is nothing much like driving a Boxster on the open road.

He went on to remind the doubters that the Boxster had outperformed all predictions, with over 120,000 sold worldwide – 'However lovely the car undoubtedly is, the sheer quantity of them out there means it isn't quite as exclusive as some owners would like.'

Duff wrote glowingly of the Boxster's dynamics: 'The Boxster feels dynamically unchanged, and that means it's still number one' – and the engine's flexibility: 'The S still has a nice, torquey power delivery, the 3.2-litre flat six engine every bit as happy to pull in high gears as it is to brush the 7,000rpm limiter in low ones.' In conclusion, Duff wrote: 'Thing is, the doubters have been proved wrong. The Boxster has sold like hot cakes and there doesn't seem to be anyone on the planet who would deny it the status of a "proper" Porsche.'

In the 2 July 2003 issue of *Autocar* a comparison test between the new BMW Z4 3.0i and the Boxster 2.7 was published. It was inevitable that the two protagonists be compared once again, especially with the BMW representing a new approach by the company to the design and engineering of its roadster.

The Z4 had slightly more power (231bhp versus 228bhp), but a lot more torque lower down in the rev range (222lb ft at 3,500rpm versus 192lb ft at 4,700rpm), which meant that the Boxster's engine had to be revved much harder to maintain station with the Z4. The standard six-speed manual gearbox (versus the Boxster 2.7's five speeder) also favoured the Z4. Driven with verve over a particularly challenging road in a Scottish forest, writer Colin Goodwin said, 'Leave the Porsche's traction control switched on and the blast through these switchbacks is ruined. The motor goes flat and your rhythm is temporarily frustrated by electronic interruptions. Switch it off and the Boxster's finely balanced chassis instantly shines.'

Goodwin found the brakes to be excellent in both cars; in normal driving the Boxster's hydraulically powered steering served up more tactile responses for the driver than did the electrically powered system of the Z4. But

pushed hard, the Z4's steering had just as much feel. Both cars topped out at 155mph (250km/h), while the Z4 was a tad quicker to 60mph from rest, taking 5.9sec against 6.3.

What was Goodwin's conclusion? He wrote:

> It's a close call, this one. Close, and one that needs a bit of breath-holding. It's all a tribute to the accumulation of small advantages such as the winning car's superior bottom-end performance, its slicker gear change, its price advantage and its more contemporary looks. But in the end, victory goes by a small but clear margin to the BMW. Seems the Boxster has hit the canvas.

Once again – beauty in motion!

The media, it seems, is quick to knock the 'tall poppy' and appears to be critical of Porsche for either not having updated the Boxster sufficiently or for not having replaced it with a new model like BMW did with the Z4. However, short model cycles have never been Porsche's way of doing business; gradual and continuous development (evolution rather than revolution) has always been the company's way and it has been no different with the Boxster. If you need proof, all you need do is look at the residuals for a Boxster compared with any of its major rivals!

Improving Upon Perfection

Fiftieth Anniversary Edition

When the Boxster was being designed, in fact from the early stages of its conception, the relationship between it and the 550 Spyder was both obvious and trumpeted by Porsche, with both cars being displayed together at the media launch. To emphasise this connection, in celebration of the fiftieth anniversary of the 550 Spyder, Porsche announced a special edition of the Boxster S, appropriately called the Fiftieth Anniversary Edition, with a limited production run of just 1,953 examples. And the subtlety of the exercise is daunting even by Porsche standards.

A lucky few have become owners of a future collectible – the Fiftieth Anniversary edition of the Boxster S.

The easiest way to identify a Fiftieth Anniversary Edition is to walk to the rear and check the exhaust outlets: this time they are stainless-steel tipped and stacked vertically with a very neat grille either side in the lower panel of the rear bumper. The 18in wheels are from the Carrera and are a five-spoke design, painted Seal Grey to harmonize with the GT Silver Metallic exterior body colour. By way of a contrast, the folding hood is Cocoa Brown in colour and the Metallic Silver and Cocoa Brown theme is

Improving Upon Perfection

carried over to the interior. It does look classy. Recognition will be made even easier if you notice the specially struck commemorative plaque that Porsche have attached to each individual car.

The sharp-eyed will notice that the Boxster S logo on the boot lid now has a polished chrome-plated finish.

The engine is your regular Boxster S unit tweaked ever so slightly to raise its output to 266bhp (an increase of just 6bhp) and the gearshift, too, has come in for some attention for a more sporting driving experience. The throw between gears has been reduced by 15 per cent and the shift lever is slightly shorter, making the gearshift quicker and more precise. For those who want the Tiptronic S option, there are steering wheel buttons to affect the gearshift when in manual mode.

Suspension ride height has been reduced by 10mm and is slightly stiffer in the settings of the springs, stabilizer bars and dampers. And just as the bright red brake calipers are a distinguishing feature of the Boxster S so, too, has the aluminium paint finished four-piston calipers on the Fiftieth Anniversary Edition become an easy recognition point.

Automatic air conditioning, the CDR-23 CD audio system and the fabulous Litronic headlights are standard equipment.

Porsche has not reached the end of its development and evolution programme for the Boxster, realizing that keeping it fresh in the minds of potential buyers is important. Prototypes of further refined examples have already been spied, as has a very pretty coupé version.

A glorious design in a relaxing setting – motoring heaven.

Boxster 2.7 Specifications

Engine:
Horizontally opposed six-cylinder ('boxer' configuration) with aluminium alloy crankcase and interchangeable cylinder heads, dual overhead camshafts per cylinder bank, four valves per cylinder, dry sump lubrication system, Bosch Digital Motor Electronic (DME) 7.2 sequential electronic fuel-injection system; from MY03 DME 7.8.

Bore:	85.5mm (3.37in)
Stroke:	78.0mm (2.83in)
Capacity:	2,687cc (151cu in)
Power:	220bhp @ 6,400rpm (from MY03 228bhp @ 6,300rpm)
Torque:	192lb ft @ 4,750rpm (same for MY03)
Specific output:	82bhp per litre (from MY03 84.85bhp)
Compression:	11.0:1

Transmission: Five-speed manual or Tiptronic S automatic

Ratios:	Manual	Automatic
1st	3.50	3.66
2nd	2.12	2.00
3rd	1.43	1.41
4th	1.09	1.00
5th	0.84	0.74
Rev	3.44	4.10
Final drive	3.56	4.02

Clutch diameter 9.45in (240mm) with two-mass flywheel
Torque converter diameter 10in (254mm) stall speed 2,400rpm

Suspension:
Front: MacPherson struts, coil springs, tubular dampers, aluminium lower A-arms, stabilizer bar.

Rear: MacPherson struts, coil springs, tubular dampers, aluminium lower lateral links and single lower trailing link, stabilizer bar.

Brakes: Hydraulic, twin-circuits with front-rear split, Bosch ABS.
Front: 11.7in (292mm) ventilated disc rotors, four-pot calipers.
Rear: 11.5in (290mm) ventilated disc rotors incorporating 6.5in (164mm) diameter brake drum for the parking brake
Total swept area: 484sq in.

Steering: Hydraulic variable power-assisted rack and pinion, overall ratio 16.9:1, lock-to-lock 3.0 turns.

Wheels:
Standard: Cast aluminium alloy, 6.0J × 16 at the front, 7.0J × 16 at the rear; tyres 205/55 ZR-16 front, 225/50 ZR-16 rear
Optional: 7.0J × 17 with 205/50 ZR-17 tyres front, 8.5J × 17 with 255/40 ZR-17 tyres rear.
Optional: 7.5J × 18 with 225/40 ZR 18 tyres front; 9J × 18 with 265/35 ZR 18 tyres rear.

Boxster 2.7 Specifications *continued*

Dimensions:	Length:	4,315mm (171.0in)
	Width:	1,780mm (70.1in)
	Height:	1,290mm (50.8in)
	Wheelbase:	2,415mm (95.2in)
	Track front:	1,455mm (57.3in) standard wheels/tyres
	Track rear:	1,508mm (59.4in) standard wheels/tyres
	Track front:	1,465mm (57.7in) optional 17in rims
	Track rear:	1,524mm (60.2in) optional 17in rims
	Fuel tank:	64 litres (14.1 Imp gal)
	Kerb weight:	1,260kg (2,756lb) manual
		1,310kg (2880lb) Tiptronic S
	Distribution:	47:53
	Drag Cd:	0.31
Performance:	Top Speed:	156mph (250km/h) manual (from MY03 157mph/253km/h)
		153mph (245km/h) Tiptronic S (from MY03 154mph/248km/h)
	0–100km/h:	6.6sec manual (MY03 6.4sec)
		7.4sec Tiptronic S (MY03 7.3sec)

Boxster S Specifications

Engine:
Horizontally opposed six-cylinder ('boxer' configuration) with aluminium alloy crankcase and interchangeable cylinder heads, dual overhead camshafts per cylinder bank, four valves per cylinder, dry sump lubrication system, Bosch Digital Motor Electronic (DME) 7.2 sequential electronic fuel-injection system. (From MY03 DME 7.8).

Bore:	93.0mm (3.37in)		
Stroke:	78.0mm (2.83in)		
Capacity:	3,179cc (151cu in)		
Power:	252bhp @ 6,250rpm (from MY03 260bhp @ 6,200rpm)		
Torque:	225lb ft @ 4,500rpm (from MY03 228lb ft @ 4,700rpm)		
Specific output:	79.19bhp per litre (from MY03 81.79bhp)		
Compression:	11.0:1		
Transmission:	Six-speed manual or Five-speed Tiptronic S automatic		
	Ratios:	Manual	Automatic
	1st	3.82	3.66
	2nd	2.20	2.00
	3rd	1.52	1.41
	4th	1.22	1.00
	5th	1.02	0.74
	6th	0.84	–

Boxster S Specifications *continued*

Rev	3.55	4.10
Final drive	3.44	3.73

Clutch diameter 9.45in (240mm) two-mass flywheel,
Torque converter diameter 10in (254mm), stall speed 2,400rpm,

Suspension:	Front:	MacPherson struts, coil springs, tubular dampers, aluminium lower A-arms, stabilizer bar.
	Rear:	MacPherson struts, coil springs, tubular dampers, aluminium lower lateral links and single lower trailing link, stabilizer bar.
Brakes:		Hydraulic, twin-circuits with front-rear split, Bosch ABS.
Front:		11.7in (292mm) ventilated disc rotors, Brembo four-pot aluminium calipers.
Rear:		11.5in (290mm) ventilated disc rotors incorporating 6.5in (164mm) diameter brake drum for the parking brake.
		Total swept area: 484sq in.
Steering:		Hydraulic variable power-assisted rack and pinion, overall ratio 16.9:1, lock-to-lock 3.0 turns.
Wheels:	Standard:	Cast aluminium alloy, 7.0J × 17 at the front, 8.5J × 17 at the rear; tyres 205/50 ZR-17 front, 255/40 ZR-17 rear.
	Optional:	7.5J × 18 with 225/40 ZR-18 tyres front, 9.0J × 18 with 265/35 ZR-18 tyres rear.
Dimensions:	Length:	4315mm (171.0in)
	Width:	1,780mm (70.1in)
	Height:	1,290mm (50.8in)
	Wheelbase:	2,415mm (95.2in)
	Track front:	1,455mm (57.3in) standard wheels/tyres
	Track rear:	1,508mm (59.4in) standard wheels/tyres
	Track front:	1,465mm (57.7in) optional 18in rims
	Track rear:	1,504mm (59.2in) ptional 18in rims
	Fuel tank:	64 litres (14.1 Imp gal)
	Kerb weight:	1,295kg (2,840lb) manual
		1,335kg (2,938lb) Tiptronic S
	Distribution:	47:53
	Drag Cd:	0.31
Performance:	Top speed	162mph (260km/h) manual (MY03 164mph/264km/h)
		159mph (255km/h) Tiptronic S (MY03 160mph/258km/h)
	Acceleration:	0–100km/h Manual 5.7sec
		Tiptronic S 6.4sec

9 Born for the USA

Success in the huge North American market has always been crucial to the financial well being of Porsche AG. After all, some 50 per cent of all production is exported to the States. Over the years it has been a close thing between the home market in Germany and North America as to which one sells the most cars. However, since the release of the Boxster, and accentuated by the release of the Cayenne, the biggest single market for Porsche cars is the good ol' US of A.

Saved by the Boxster

As has been recounted elsewhere in this book, Porsche had been at its lowest ebb for many years when in 1993 it displayed the Boxster concept car at the Detroit Motor Show. Something like a mere 3,700 cars were sold in the USA that year! As Bob Carlson, General Manager, Public Relations at Porsche Cars North America (PCNA), said to me:

> We had our display in a corner of one of the halls at Detroit – we could not afford anything extravagant – and when Dr Wiedeking unveiled the car I was standing next to a lady whom I respect highly, Denise McCluggage. In fact I deliberately went and stood next to her, as I believed she was a very

By 1995 both the 968 and 928 had been discontinued from the Porsche programme, leaving just the 1993 edition 911 to carry the flame for the company until the arrival of the Boxster.

Not somewhere west of Laramie but it might be close.

The silhouette of a future classic sports car.

Born for the USA

accurate bell-weather as to how successful the styling might be. Anyway, when the covers were taken off she quietly said to me 'You guys have got it!' I knew then that we were on to a winner. Her comment was repeated several times by many other industry people during that hectic day.

McCluggage was a respected motoring journalist and racer, being the first female racing driver in America, where she was successful in many events driving the 550 Spyder among a wide range of other cars.

An interesting insight to the tight security enforced by the company was the total secrecy of the car's styling. Only one or two executives at the top of PCNA had seen it. Certainly Carlson had not. He was contacted by the editor of the hugely influential (in America) *Autoweek* publication, who asked him, 'Is it worth saving the front cover for your car?' Carlson responded in the affirmative and, when the car was unveiled and photos taken, that issue of *Autoweek* was a massive sell-out, so keen were readers to know about the new sports car from Porsche.

As Carlson commented, 'All the signs were looking good! That display at Detroit '93 was a very real turning point in the company's history in my opinion.'

In retrospect, the Boxster concept car was what he described as 'something of a trial balloon' to test the reaction from both the media and the public on the potential for the future Porsche.

In all the hype and hysteria that surrounded the Boxster many people overlooked the importance of the Type 993 Porsche 911. According to Carlson:

> The Boxster is generally credited with saving the company and that cannot be denied, as it was a critically important new car for us. But it was the 993 that really began our climb back from the abyss and generated the cash flow to sustain us until the 986 was ready for the market. You must also remember that the Types 968 and 928 were

With looks like this you can understand why the American buyers bought the Boxster in large numbers consistently.

Born for the USA

Improvements included the new multi-function read-out in the lower arc of the tachometer face.

discontinued in 1995, so for a two-year period the 993 was all we had. Whilst it looked like the old 964, underneath significant changes were made that made it a far more accessible vehicle for enthusiast drivers; it was far less intimidating to drive very fast.

Where the 993 laid the foundation for today's success, it was the Boxster that gave the company greater impetus in the market place and added significantly to the company's sale volumes and convinced the dealers to invest in their future, a decision that was emphasized and confirmed by the arrival of the Cayenne.

According to Carlson, in 1986 PCNA sold in the vicinity of 30,000 vehicles, 20,000 of which were 944s, a car that was incredibly successful for Porsche internationally. But, as he said, along came 1987 and things went pear-shaped:

> There was the Stock Market crash that coincided with the Deutsche Mark being devalued against the American dollar and here we were with what were perceived as old products that suddenly were far more expensive than previously and, more importantly, were now significantly more expensive against competitors like the Mazda RX-7 and Nissan 300ZX. It was the beginning of a dangerous downward spiral for Porsche.

From Porsche's perspective, the sports car market has always been somewhat volatile because the clients expect to have the latest and greatest. At that point in its history, Porsche had neither and almost paid the price.

This situation was exacerbated by the fact that Porsche rarely did a completely new car. You could almost count them on one hand: Boxster/996, 928, 924, 914, 911, 356 and some racers. In the long-held tradition of the company, once a new model had been released it then evolved gradually over many years – there was no revolution at Porsche, unlike some manufacturers of sports cars that borrow components from humdrum mainstream family cars at will and turn out completely new models every four years, sometimes fewer. Each of these Porsche models had a very long production life and were made in a number of series that coincided with technical improvements first, and styling upgrades as a (relatively) minor issue.

The Boxster has been a typical case in point, having gone through several iterations since its release in late 1996 as a 1997 model year. There have been many significant technical advances, not the least of which was the release of the Boxster S, but you'd be hard pressed to pick the model year differences, so subtle are they. This has contrasted markedly with BMW and Mercedes-Benz, which have both released completely new editions of their sports cars – Z4 and new SLK respectively – in a far shorter timeframe than Porsche can afford to match. As Carlson commented, 'Porsche is still a niche manufacturer and while we have achieved some economies of scale with the component sharing between the 986 and 996, our volumes are still tiny, and our cars still have a large handmade aura about them.'

While Porsche rarely displays concept cars as such, the circumstances at the time dictated a new strategy and with the 1993 Detroit Motor Show coming it made sense for the

The centre console (ex-911) now has the Porsche Communication Module (PCM) that includes the sat-nav system displayed.

company to show its hand to some extent in its most important export market. Such was the reaction to the unveiling that between 1993 and the car's release in America in January 1997 more than 10,000 firm orders were placed with the various dealers around the nation. That represented at least two years' production and was virtually money in the bank for PCNA and Porsche AG.

The 2.7-litre Boxster might only have one exhaust outlet but it is a decent size.

127

The revised and slightly more aggressive bumpers are clearly visible on both cars here.

Unlike previous-generation Porsches, where there had to be several versions of the car to meet often widely differing safety and emission requirements – Europe was different from America, which was different from Japan, which was different from Australia, and so on – for the new generation of water-cooled engines only one global version was manufactured. This simplified the whole design and manufacturing processes.

Porsche chose to introduce the Boxster to the American public at the Greater Los Angeles Auto Show on 3 January 1997. In his speech, PCNA President Fred Schwab said:

> The public demanded we build this car. The Boxster's look captured the imagination of young and old, Porsche owners and aspirants, as well as many who had never even considered a Porsche.

And we had to build it to round out our sports car line-up. We wanted an entry-level Porsche that would complement the incomparable and legendary 911, as well as offering pure sports car attributes like fun driving pleasure, outstanding performance and solid roadholding. We have achieved all of these goals in the 1997 Porsche Boxster.

For the North American market the new Boxster was extremely well equipped. Creature comforts like air conditioning, power windows and mirrors, electric seat back adjustment, leather-facing surfaces on the seats, AM/FM/cassette stereo system and an electrically powered hood that opened or closed in 12 seconds were all standard. The price, and this was the most important of the suggestions from PCNA in the lead-up to its release, was to be under $40,000. In the event, it came in just $20 under! Nevertheless, the Boxster was more expensive than the BMW Z3 and Mercedes-Benz SLK.

Schwab continued by saying, 'An entry-level Porsche in price but, obviously, not in specification. This is a true Porsche, one whose heritage is directly linked to the great early Porsche roadsters.'

In February 1997, mid-winter, Porsche invited up to 100 members of the press to the release that was held in Wig Wam, near Phoenix, Arizona. The actual technical presentation was carried out in the conference centre that was formerly part of the Goodyear Tyre and Rubber Company facility in the desert. Not far away from there was the Phoenix International Raceway, where on the second day the press was let loose in the Boxster to judge for itself just how much a Porsche this newcomer really was.

The eulogies flowed in the press across the nation for weeks and months afterwards.

The Boxster was the predicator of many new developments in the Porsche fraternity in America. Not only did it significantly revitalize the dealer network, but also Porsche Cars North America planned a bigger future for itself. At the time of the Boxster's release the company was headquartered in Reno, Nevada, somewhat off the beaten business track even in America. A move was planned eastwards and in 1998 it relocated to new premises in Atlanta, Georgia.

Most important of all, however, was the effect of the car on the dealers. Until the Boxster many Porsche dealers were multi-franchised with often an American brand paired with European and Japanese brands, often on the same showroom floor. Because the volume of business with Porsche was minuscule at the time, the dealer would have a 911 or a 968 or perhaps a 928 tucked away in a corner of the showroom, and no specialist Porsche sales staff. A complete revamp of the network took place and with the increased sales volume and turnover, dealer principals were prepared to make the necessary investment of building a separate and exclusive showroom and associated facilities befitting the purchase of one of the world's premier brands. Today the company has 194 dealers in its national network and more than a third of them have a dedicated Porsche facility with enthusiastic sales staff, that number growing with the advent and success of the AWD Cayenne.

Between January 1997 and February 2004 PCNA sold more than 71,400 Boxsters, made up of 53,200 Boxster and 18,244 Boxster Ss. This was certainly a good effort considering what is available to the American buyer by way of sports cars.

Clearly seen here is the rearrangement of functions with the digital speed read-out directly below the analogue speedometer; multi-function display below the tachometer; oil level below the combination dial.

10 And Now for Something a Little Different, a Little Faster

Competition, that most public of test arenas, is not on the agenda for the Boxster. Porsche has decreed that all factory competition efforts will be directed through its traditional racecar, the 911. That is why there has never been a very high performance version of the Boxster on offer from Porsche AG. And further to that, despite the fact that some cynics have described the Boxster as a poor man's 911, and many owners have bought Boxsters on their way to a 911, the Boxster stands on its own set of alloy wheels as a true Porsche.

But that does not mean that wealthy Porsche enthusiasts cannot indulge their whims and desires with a more powerful Boxster. From Day One of the Boxster's life people have been complaining about its lack of power, or at least the feeling of a lack of power. Even those who have the 260bhp Boxster S still crave more power.

RUF Automobiles

There is an answer to their prayers and it comes from a variety of after-market specialists who all worship Porsches. The first of these companies that we will look at is in Pfaffen-

Aggressive, sexy, powerful – the going-away view of the RUF 3600 S Boxster. (Photograph courtesy of RUF)

The RUF 3600 S quietly cruising one of the minor roads in its beautiful native Bavaria. Note the aggressive, perhaps exaggerated, front spoiler. (Photograph courtesy of RUF)

hausen, a town near Munich in Bavaria. It is a small manufacturer by the name of RUF Automobiles GmbH, and it is owned and run by Alois Ruf. Alois Ruf Senior first started the business back in 1939, but until 1976 it was a small garage looking after the servicing of various makes, including Porsche. Why was 1976 such a seminal year for RUF? It was the year in which Porsche introduced its 911 Turbo. In 1977 RUF offered for the first time a RUF-modified high-performance 911 based on the factory's Turbo. The RUF version, however, produced 300bhp (40bhp more than standard) from an enlarged 3.3-litre air-cooled flat six. Its acceleration was electrifying and quickly established RUF as a quality modifier of Porsches. In 1981 RUF was the first Porsche tuner to offer the 911 Turbo with a five-speed gearbox, while in 1983 came the really big breakthrough for RUF with the release of the 911 BTR that had a 374bhp version of the flat-six engine, the five-speed gearbox. Each car was carefully crafted by hand, starting with a bare bodyshell. Throughout the 1980s and 1990s RUF offered its discerning clients ever more powerful versions of the various 911 models, quite possibly the most memorable being the CTR with its brutal twin-turbo engine producing 409bhp. It lapped the famous Nardo circuit in Italy at 213mph (342km/h).

RUF has been a manufacturer in its own right under the requirements of the German TÜV organization since 1981, making between twenty-five and thirty cars each year. The company buys each car from Porsche AG as a body-in-white and creates the final product for each client, each RUF Porsche being virtually custom-made.

The release in 1997 of the next generation 986 and 996 Porsches opened new possibilities for RUF, especially with the Boxster that was always considered somewhat underpowered. This problem was solved when RUF displayed the 310bhp Boxster 3400 S at the 1999 Essen Motor Show. It was exactly what the company's clientele were looking for!

In creating the RUF 3600 S the company fits the 3.6-litre water-cooled flat six from the 996 range into the Boxster's mid-engine bay. Because the 3.6 is slightly taller than the standard 3.2 engine, RUF engineers mount it slightly lower in the bay to avoid having to redesign the intake system, thus avoiding

And Now for Something a Little Different, a Little Faster

Higher speeds require greater cooling of the engine and brakes – note the huge air scoops either side of the spoiler. (Photograph courtesy of RUF)

expensive type approval certification – they can use Porsche's. For the same reason the catalytic converters are positioned in exactly the same place relative to the exhaust ports as on a 996, although the actual exhaust outlets are higher and exit through the rear bumper, just under the tail lights. Sexy!

A Carrera clutch is substituted for the Boxster's, but the rest of the driveline is pure Boxster S. The four-wheel disc braking system is from the Boxster S, too, but with the front calipers now painted black and carrying the RUF logo; the suspension, however, is RUF tweaked and you can order 19in wheels fitted with Pirelli Asimmetrico high-performance tyres.

Boxster enthusiasts would love the company's latest creation, the Boxster 3600 S, because in one car it embraces all that they desire: more power (345bhp), more torque (273lb ft), faster acceleration (0–100km/h in 5.1sec) and a faster maximum speed (173mph/278km/h).

The majority of Porsche modifiers are to be found in Germany, although many of them have direct connections through agents to the United Kingdom and United States markets.

TechArt

TechArt Automobildesign is another quality after-market company that can provide Boxster owners with almost whatever their fancy chooses, whether that be simple things like specially designed spoilers or alloy wheels, or more serious additions to the chassis and engine. For example, TechArt will also carry out a 3.6-litre conversion, adding special pistons, con rods and crankshaft together with a

TechArt, like most after-market suppliers to Boxster owners, offers interesting aerodynamic packages. This one has wider sills and relocated air scoops in the extended rear wings. (Photograph courtesy of TechArt)

modified induction system – special air filter system, aluminium manifold – sports camshafts and redesigned stainless steel exhaust manifolds. The ECU is recalibrated to match these changes to the engine's specifications so that it now develops 330bhp of power and 380 Nm of torque. Performance is enhanced to the tune of a maximum speed of 176mph (282km/h) and the 0–100km/h acceleration run takes just 4.9sec.

The company recommends that owners fit TechArt-designed 'body styling components' – company speak for redesigned spoilers front, side and rear – to improve further the Boxster's high-speed stability. TechArt offers two front spoiler designs, both aimed at the dual purpose of aiding stability by reducing lift on the nose, and also improving the aesthetics of the sports car. The side skirts make the car look lower and longer, while the air ducts on the rear wings have been enlarged to improve airflow to the engine. At the rear, the wing is no longer retractable and now adds to the Boxster's appearance and again reduces the airlift at high speeds.

Being a design company, TechArt offers Boxster owners a wide range of exclusively designed alloy wheels. They are possibly best known for their Formula alloys that are an extremely light one-piece design with five spokes.

The company's expertise can also be employed in modifying the interior with individually selected leathers, seats and steering wheels, as well as customized sound systems.

Following the success of its 'wide-bodied' 911 Carrera from the 996 range, the company now offers Boxster clients the same option. New guards front and rear add some 8mm to

A slightly less extreme aero package but with a lowered suspension and wider than standard wheels. All that is missing is the bass exhaust note. (Photograph courtesy of TechArt)

A full leather interior is available for those who desire (and can afford) the best. Included is a very thick-rimmed sports steering wheel. (Photograph courtesy of TechArt)

And Now for Something a Little Different, a Little Faster

The aggressive rear of a TechArt-modified Boxster. The wheels in particular look great. This is the 3.6-litre 320bhp conversion capable of 176mph. (Photograph courtesy of TechArt)

the overall width of the car, but, more importantly, create more space under the wheel arches for larger wheels and tyres as well as further improving the car's aerodynamic performance. Accompanying this body alteration comes TechArt-designed Champion alloy wheels, 8.5J × 18 at the front and 11J × 18 at the rear with 225/40 ZR 18 and 285/30 ZR 18 Continental ContiSportContact high-speed tyres. Also available with this conversion is the TechArt height-adjustable sports suspension that can lower the car by between 20 and 35mm.

TechArt has been in the Porsche modifying business for many years, starting off back in 1987 when two colleagues, Thomas Behringer and Matthias Krauss, began doing interior upgrades for the 911 as well as on various BMWs and Mercedes-Benz. Initially the company was based in Fellbach, a town some 10km to the east of Stuttgart, with just five employees. Today the company is based in Leonberg to the west of Stuttgart and it employs fifty people.

Gemballa

For more than twenty-five years Uwe Gemballa has been tuning – don't you just love that word in its German context? – Porsches at the highest level. The business was started in 1979, the main activity then being the upgrading of interiors of Volkswagens, BMWs as well as Porsches. It was not a giant step from there to being able to offer clients the complete package, customized interior with a mechanical makeover, the only limiting factor being the depth of the client's resources. Gemballa GmbH is now one of the leading purveyors of a wide range of equipment with which to personalize your Porsche.

The Gemballa portfolio today covers the 911 and Cayenne as well as the Boxster. The

And Now for Something a Little Different, a Little Faster

Gemballa GmbH offers a wide range of package modifications for the Boxster. This is its GTR EVO. (Photograph courtesy of Gemballa)

new Cayenne, for example, is available in four versions culminating in the GT 700 that boasts (as its badge suggests) a massive 700bhp at 6,050rpm and a huge 1,050 Nm of torque at 3,500rpm. This *Wunderwagen* will blast from 0–100km/h in a mere 4.5sec, to 200km/h in a staggering 13.8sec and run to 180mph (289km/h).

If the 911 is your Porsche, Gemballa can raise your adrenalin levels with three offerings, beginning with the GTR 550 Cabrio that has 520bhp at 7,050rpm and zips from 0–100km/h in 3.9sec with a maximum of 196 mph (315km/h) – what a hairdryer! The GTR 600 has 600bhp at 7,120rpm at its disposal, blasts from 0–100km/h in 3.7sec on its way to a time of 10.6sec for the 200km/h and a maximum speed of 205mph (330km/h). The top 911, the GTR 650 EVO, boasts no less than 650bhp at 7,280rpm and a whopping 950 Nm of torque to register times of 3.5sec and 9.8sec for the 0–100 and 200km/h runs and a maximum of 214mph (345km/h).

For Boxster S owners the excitement level rises to the Roadster GTR 500 EVO that features a bi-turbocharged 3.6-litre engine that produces a mighty 500bhp at 6,980rpm and 680 Nm of torque at 5,100rpm. Its maximum speed is quoted by Gemballa as 193mph (310km/h), and it is able to run the 0–100km/h sprint in 4.0sec and on to 200km/h in just 11.5sec. The GTR 500 EVO is no shrinking violet – you could never travel unobserved in one. It features a full

And Now for Something a Little Different, a Little Faster

What a beautiful sight! The view under the engine cover of the Gemballa Boxster. (Photograph courtesy of Gemballa)

aerodynamic kit that includes front and rear wing extensions to cover the wide 235/35 front and 315/25 Yokohama tyres on Gemballa 19in alloy multi-spoked racing wheels, front air-dam from the GT2 EVO, side skirts with a lower air channel to help cool the rear brakes and take heat away from the turbochargers, rear spoiler with a black carbon fibre wing, a front bonnet from the 911 GT and two large exhaust outlets coming through the rear bumper.

Naturally, there are many component upgrades to go with the significantly increased power and performance. In addition to the two KKK turbochargers, the engine has sports catalysts, air filters and a customized exhaust

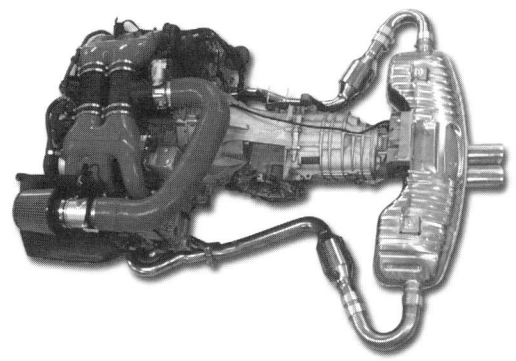

One of the options available from Gemballa includes a 3.9-litre version of the water-cooled boxer six-cylinder engine. All development work was carried out by Gemballa's own R&D staff. (Photograph courtesy of Gemballa)

For Boxster enthusiasts wanting the ultimate power and performance thrill, Gemballa offers the 3.6-litre twin-turbo six. (Photograph courtesy of Gemballa)

And Now for Something a Little Different, a Little Faster

Guess what the 500 stands for? And I wonder how beautiful the exhaust note from those twin outlets would sound? (Photograph courtesy of Gemballa)

system; then there is the Gemballa-developed (from racing experience with the 911) suspension and braking systems, the latter being based on huge 380mm diameter Brembo disc rotors with eight-piston calipers. Part of the engine upgrade includes a deeper oil pan (it has an extra 1 litre of oil) with baffles to prevent the loss of oil pressure under severe cornering loads.

All modified Gemballa engines feature an in-house developed special lightweight flywheel, while the clutch is a Sachs unit developed to Gemballa specifications.

Gemballa has added to its stable the Boxster Roadster GT with a massive 3.9-litre boxer six-cylinder engine. It uses a 996 Carrera crankshaft and forged Mahle pistons mated with 100mm diameter cylinder liners that incorporate metal tubes to reinforce the block so as to ensure a long service life. Power output is a modest 375–380bhp at 6,000rpm, but, as Uwe Gemballa said, 'It's the torque that is most impressive with this engine at around 420 Nm.'

And, as Uwe Gemballa continued, 'We will never carry out a part-modification; we will never do just an engine, for example, even though the client is willing to pay. No, our philosophy is that our clients must buy the complete package to ensure the product is capable of meeting our exacting standards.'

To promote the company's technical developments, Uwe Gemballa has proved his mod-

And Now for Something a Little Different, a Little Faster

A Gemballa-modified interior with leather upholstered sports seats, dashboard, console and steering wheel; also note the dimpled foot pedals for better grip. (Photograph courtesy of Gemballa)

ifications in the most intense and public way possible, that of competition against his rivals. On 22 August 2001, a Gemballa-modified 911 GTR 600 set a new lap record for its class on the famous Nürburgring-Nordschleife circuit of 7:32.5sec, a time that still stands today. Interestingly, the previous year at the Nurburgring the Gemballa GTR 600 set the lap record for its class at 7:44.7sec, which means that in the space of just one year the company has broken its own record by an amazing 12.2sec!

The company also set a new record at the Hockenheim circuit in July 2003, in a Gemballa GTR 600 EVO, when it lapped at 1:07.9sec competing in the 'super-fast class'.

Based in the town of Leonberg (same as TechArt) Gemballa has recently undergone a major expansion of its facilities that includes a spacious showroom, a state-of-the-art technical department, a design and R&D division, spare parts and corporate offices. 'This is my way of saying I am confident of the future of Porsche and my association with Porsche,' said Uwe Gemballa. The company has a staff of just thirty people, all dedicated Porsche enthusiasts. Being able to modify your Boxster using Gemballa-developed equipment is not limited to Germany, however, because the company has a network of agencies around the world.

Turbo Tuning Peitz

Another of the German tuners is Turbo Tuning Peitz or TTP, as it is known in the industry. Based in Kolbermoor, between Munich and Rosenheim off the A8 Munich-Salzburg autobahn, it is possibly the only tuning company that makes the Boxster go faster, both in acceleration and maximum speed, using turbocharger technology. For owners of an early Boxster with the 2.5-litre engine, TTP offers two routes to added power and performance. The first is a simple recalibration of the ECU together with a carbon-fibre airbox with sports air filter, exhaust headers and a specially fabricated stainless steel exhaust system which liberates a further 25bhp, giving the driver access now to 229bhp at 6,200rpm and 265 Nm of torque at a high 5,900rpm. If that is not enough, the company offers a twin-turbo bolt-on conversion that can be carried out without taking the engine out of the engine

And Now for Something a Little Different, a Little Faster

Above The smooth lines of the Boxster are enhanced by TTP's aero kit and multi-spoked road wheels. (Photograph courtesy of TTP)

Below Like its rivals, TTP has developed a deeper and more aggressive front spoiler to enhance the sports car's aero performance. (Photograph courtesy of TTP)

And Now for Something a Little Different, a Little Faster

TTP's 3.6-litre twin-turbo boxer engine. It is a marvel of packaging as the available space in the Boxster's engine bay is not that great. (Photograph courtesy of TTP)

bay! The installation involves two T25 Garret turbochargers, water intercooler plus the usual ECU recalibration along with a specially fabricated set of exhaust headers and exhaust system. The gains here are considerable, the Boxster now having 290bhp at 5,800rpm and a whopping 400 Nm of torque at 4,900rpm to push it along.

TTP offers similar options for both the 2.7-litre Boxster and 3.2-litre Boxster S. The ECU recalibration option liberates a further 25bhp in each case (now to 253bhp and 285bhp respectively), while the twin-turbo option takes the 2.7 up to 330bhp at 5,800rpm and 430 Nm at 5,100rpm and the 3.2 up to 390bhp and 510 Nm at 5,900 and 5,100rpm respectively. With these conversions the extent is a little more comprehensive, consisting of twin T25 KKK turbochargers for the 2.7 and K16s for the 3.2, with a new intake system and the specially fabricated exhaust system plus the water spray intercooler to keep the temperature of the incoming mixture within predetermined limits to prevent detonation.

TTP also offers two Boxster versions with a 3.6-litre engine, although it is not a direct 996 transplant but rather a modified 986 block with 996 crankshaft, con rods and pistons fitted. With the low-key TTP modifications – ECU recalibration, stainless steel exhaust system plus a sports catalytic converter – it produces 320bhp at 6,800rpm and 380 Nm of torque at 5,000rpm with the ignition cut-out set at 7,300rpm. However, when equipped with the twin-turbo conversion the power is hiked to a massive 450bhp and torque to a mind-blowing 620 Nm at 6,400 and 4,550rpm respectively. The engine upgrade is extremely comprehensive this time, comprising two K24 turbo units along with TTP's ECU modifications, special intake and exhaust systems, lowered compression ratio, fully machined cylinder heads, forged crankshaft and pistons, water intercooler, high capacity oil cooler and a reinforced clutch.

It is a measure of the built-in strength of the Boxster gearbox that it can take this amount of power and torque without apparent ill effects. The use of the gearbox from a GT3, for example, is precluded by the fact that the flange between the engine and gearbox is different and, importantly, its direction of rotation is the reverse of what is required in a mid-engined configuration.

Where braking is concerned TTP offer upgrades for early Boxsters to Boxster S specifications and on the later models the two-piece 330mm rotors and calipers from the 993

Turbo. As well, it is possible for TTP to fit the 996 GT2/GT3 front suspension so that the original GT3 four-piston calipers can be fitted or the original GT2 six-piston with 350mm diameter rotors if serious work is envisaged.

TTP have a number of manufacturers which supply wheels for its conversions; the most often used are those from Dynatech, 8 × 18in at the front and 9 × 18in at the rear, usually with Dunlop tyres. However, the company is flexible in these issues as long as the supplier meets the very strict quality requirements of TTP.

On the subject of air-cooled versus water-cooled Porsche engines, the CEO of TTP, Ferdinand Pietz, commented:

> You cannot directly compare the two engines. The air-cooled was developed for over thirty years and had a potential for up to 1,000bhp (962 Group C cars), but for normal road use you don't need such high power.
>
> The water-cooled engine is in the meantime now reliable, powerful, quiet and is able to pass all emission controls. In the beginning there were problems, especially in the 3.4-litre engine, with the pistons running in the bores. In a hard-driven car with untoughened engines you had too much friction between the piston and bore, and they had a problem with the quality of the cast aluminium blocks and cylinder heads. These problems are well in the past, but they are the reason why a lot of people with poor knowledge will tell you that the water-cooled engine is no good.
>
> The water-cooled engine is perfect and when a tuner does his homework the engine is good for a reliable 500bhp and shows a better temperature diagram inside than the air-cooled – otherwise a bolt-on 390bhp 3.2 would never work!

Turbo Tuning Pietz has its roots in the Lotec racing team from the 1980s, a team that was very successful and gained infamy through its turbocharging developments of Mercedes-Benz and Ferrari automobiles. The driving force behind these developments was Ferdinand Pietz. So successful were the Pietz-developed cars that the Ferrari Testa Rossa-based test car – the Lotec Colani test D'oro – established several world records for road sports cars in 1991.

Since then, Pietz has continued his development of twin-turbocharged high-performance automobiles and concentrated mainly on Porsches as the basis for his business. Testimony to his prowess has been the recognition of his work by the *sport auto* magazine readership, which voted his TTP-modified Porsches as the top in their category – *sport auto* awards were won in 1997, 1998, 2001 and 2002.

In November 2000 the world record was set at the Nürburgring with a lap time of 7:44min in a Gemballa 911 GT3 turbo that was powered by a TTP-developed engine. As Ferdinand Pietz said, 'We can provide our tuning concepts to any Porsche vehicle, whether mid- or rear-engined, coupé or cabrio, Tiptronic or manual, two-wheel drive or AWD.'

TTP has invested heavily in the necessary equipment to meet all emission regulations no matter how powerful the engine may be – its test stand for engines incorporates the exhaust gas analysis and application systems to meet Euro 3 and Euro 4 standards.

Strosek Auto Design

Possibly the least extreme of the well-known Porsche modifiers is Strosek Auto Design, which is located in the town of Utting on the shore of *Ammersee* (Lake Ammer in English), between München and the Alps. It really is picture-book scenery and an ideal place in many ways for creative thought. It is quite some way off the proverbial beaten track, although at weekends and on holidays the good burghers of München drive south to their summer villas on the shores of the lake.

The company is named after its creator, Vittorio Strosek, who was born in Germany to an

And Now for Something a Little Different, a Little Faster

Vittorio Strosek prefers restrained modifications to the Boxster despite a history of extrovert designs for other clients.

Italian father. A graduate of the Bergische University in Wuppertal, Strosek worked with Luigi Colani for a year – now there is a man with seriously way-out ideas! – before venturing out on his own as an independent designer in 1972 when he founded the Auto Mobil Design Studio. A decade later Strosek relocated to Utting and opened Strosek Auto Design, with one of his first clients being Willi Koenig, who gained considerable fame (or should that be infamy?) for his sometimes outrageous modifications to various Ferraris during the 1980s. At the same time, Strosek and Koenig became internationally renowned for the wild 911s that wore Strosek-designed body modifications by way of new bumpers and much-needed aerodynamic addenda.

Vittorio Strosek was one of the first to develop a programme of mild modifications for the 928 – which he termed 'the stepchild of the Porsche range' – comprising aerodynamic improvements as well as a subtle retuning of the chassis and wheels and tyres. Success here brought 911 clients to Utting and now, with the Boxster, a far wider circle of Porsche owners are seeking Strosek's (mostly) cosmetic upgrades. Strosek's aerodynamic improvements have apparently not gone unnoticed by Porsche; according to Strosek, Porsche copied the rear diffuser for the S.

Strosek's cosmetic improvements are also aerodynamic with superior airflow to the radiators, brakes and under the Boxster.

While most clients have been more than happy with the improved aerodynamics and mild wheel-and-tyre modifications, Strosek can, in collaboration with specialist Porsche engine tuners, provide varying degrees of additional brio for the Boxster. It all depends on your needs and wants – and ability to afford.

FVD

Another tuning company is FVD from Unkirk in Germany. Their British distributor, G-Force Motorsport located in Aylesbury, Buckinghamshire, is one of England's largest and most successful Porsche specialists, having serviced the racing programme of founder John Greasley for many years. The company's expertise extends from simple MOT inspections through to full-blown circuit upgrades to Le Mans style competition support for any model from the 1960s to today's 996 and Boxsters.

As with any modification programme, it all depends on what you want to achieve – you should be crystal clear on this – and how much you want to pay. With G-Force, you can simply install special seats that are designed for a more body-hugging experience, or a new steering wheel or new faces for the instruments. Or you can invest more serious money in engine, suspension, chassis and aerodynamic improvements. Kits can be supplied to boost the power of the 2.5-litre Boxster engine to 220bhp by a revision of the DME system, sports air filter and an exhaust header system (this is much like the work done by Strosek, TTP and others), while the 2.7 can be boosted to 235bhp and the 3.2

And Now for Something a Little Different, a Little Faster

up to 265bhp by this method. If you want more capacity, G-Force can supply an ex-996 3.4-litre boxer engine that will bolt straight in and give you access to 300bhp and more torque. If you want some serious power, the company can offer a twin-turbo conversion that uses the latest in turbo technology and parts from the GT2 (to ensure reliability and service) that will yield 350bhp and give the Boxster electrifying acceleration.

The company has a full range of suspension kits as well as camber plates that have been milled from a solid aluminium billet. These replace the soft rubber bushing at the top of the suspension strut and allow up to 6 degrees of negative camber. Braking system upgrades include the fitting of the full GT3 system.

ROOCK North America

In the USA, the small, family-owned company of ROOCK North America specializes in making your Porsche go faster. The company is located on the Alpharetta Highway in Roswell, just north of Atlanta.

The parent company was founded in 1984 in Leverkusen near Cologne, Germany, by Fabian and Michael Roock, with the aim of repairing and tuning Porsches. They were successful and in 1990 set up ROOCK Motorsport to challenge the best in the Porsche tuning business on their own turf.

Again, they were successful. During their impressive European racing career, including the prestigious Porsche Carrera Cup and Supercup series, the ROOCK Porsche racing team claimed five championships and over thirty individual first places. In 1996, the team took first place in their division at the crown jewel of all racing events, the 24 Hours of Le Mans, and in 1997 and 1999 at the 24 Hours of Daytona.

ROOCK then moved its successful European racing team to the USA, to Road Atlanta raceway (home of the Petite Le Mans) in Braselton, Georgia, where it competed in the American Le Mans Series as well as establishing ROOCK North America. The team finished second in the ALMS in both 2000 and 2001. In that year Fabian Roock

The quality of the ROOCK conversion is evident here. Such conversions are naturally expensive, but Boxster owners looking for a superior driving experience are prepared to pay.

ROOCK provides Boxster owners with a complete package – aerodynamic body attachments, wheels and tyres, suspension, brakes and engine.

decided to focus his business entirely on developing performance systems for Porsches in-house and to forgo his racing activities for the time being.

The company offers two versions of the Boxster for those who demand more from their car, the Boxster 310 and 340. Both models are an interesting cocktail of 986 and 996 components. The slightly less powerful Boxster 310 comes with the 3.4-litre version of the 996 water-cooled flat six-cylinder engine, which has a modified engine ECU and sports exhaust headers, and a free-flowing exhaust system with altered catalytic converters together with an improved intake system to generate 310bhp and 273lb ft of torque. The Boxster 340 uses the 3.6-litre version of the 996 boxer engine with similar modifications to the 310. The result is 340bhp at 6,800rpm and an acceleration time from 0–60mph in 4.9sec and a maximum speed of 180mph (290km/h).

Included in the upgrading of the Boxster are such key items as ROOCK's Sports suspension system that utilizes Bilstein springs; the braking system is derived from the 996 Carrera with 330mm ventilated rotors front and rear; a GT3 body lit comprising front bumper, side skirt and rear spoiler and diffuser; and ROOCK competition five-spoke, two-part forged aluminium wheels that are 9 × 18in at the front, 10 × 18in at the rear with 225/40 and 265/35 tyres respectively. As Fabian Roock said, 'We've taken an already great Porsche product and made it even better. It's a definite head turner!'

11 New Production Technology

Production methods at Porsche's Stuttgart-Zuffenhausen plant over the decades prior to the arrival of Wendelin Wiedeking and the 986/996 programmes could best be described as 'traditional'. In today's parlance they were 'labour intensive', with little evidence of just-in-time stock control and no, repeat no, robots. Each 911 was carefully and expensively built on its own production line as was the earlier 928. The 924/944/968 family of sports coupés and cabrios did enjoy a more modern assembly process, but they were assembled under contract by Audi at the ex-NSU factory in Neckarsulm for much of their production life – the 968 was built at Stuttgart-Zuffenhausen only near the end of its time.

Moving with the Times

For Porsche to remain an independent maker of sports cars and to be profitable, the old techniques had to be consigned to the history books. It was imperative that new technology be embraced and used to the company's benefit in every way possible. Despite what the old traditionalists might think, but would not want

The charismatic President and CEO of Porsche, Dr Wiedeking was a production specialist who completely reorganized the company and sanctioned the 986/996 programme.

New Production Technology

Far to the north of Stuttgart lies the town of Uusikaupunki in Finland where Porsche's partner company Valmet is located. (Photograph courtesy of Valmet)

to admit, the fact is that with today's sophisticated technology the production of particular components need not be by hand. Robots can be programmed to carry out amazingly complex tasks and do them time after time with unerring accuracy. Not even the best craftsman could do that!

It was not only in the area of the physical production of a Porsche that change had to be made – it needed to be made as well (and probably more importantly) in the way in which a new model was conceived and developed. In other words, from fundamental principles forward. Not an easy task in any company, but one that Porsche had to face and conquer.

Over the past decade the buzz phrase has been 'simultaneous engineering'. Basically this means that any department within the company, from Styling to Engineering and all its disciplines to Production, Purchasing, Marketing, Service and so on, work together with the project leader(s) to design-in from the beginning the new cost-effective design and manufacturing processes that make the new car easier (and therefore less expensive) to build in the first place and less expensive for the owner to maintain over the years. They are not added on as the design progresses through the various departments in the company, one after another, as was the case previously. As the project expands and progresses, supplier partner companies' representatives are added to the team so that the whole process becomes integrated and cohesive.

Horst Marchant, Board Member for Research and Development at the time that the Boxster was conceived (he has since retired) was quoted as saying, 'We have become more scientific in the way we work. Maybe

Porsche invested heavily in new production technologies including robotized welding operations for the assembly of the body. This has significantly reduced the time and cost of production.

this is not always as exciting as it used to be, but the final results are really impressive.'

The arrival of Wendelin Wiedeking saw a sea change take place within Porsche, a change that was to have far-reaching ramifications for the company, its products, its employees and its future. As Wiedeking said, 'In the first place we made the company significantly leaner and more flexible by cutting the hierarchical levels from six to four and by shedding around 1,800 jobs throughout the group – in a socially acceptable way. Moreover, series that were negatively impacting our financial statements were discontinued.'

He went on to say, 'In the second stage, with the aim of securing the long-term sustainability of Porsche, we radically modernized the outmoded production and resolutely trimmed it to achieve the highest efficiency. All process were put under the microscope.'

Furthermore, he added, 'We had already decided in the planning phase to produce the two future series 986 and 996 on the one production line. Only in this way was it possible to make use of synergies and to keep our production lean, flexible and efficient. The constructional conditions for extensive joint production were therefore put in place right from the development stage.'

By doing this Wiedeking not only restructured the way the company operated, he also flattened the management structure to shorten the lines of both communication and responsibilities. He also did what many German managers would have described as the unthinkable – he approached the Japanese for solutions to his problems. Now, while the Japanese might not be innovative in their design of an automobile (they tend to be

Valmet, too, has similarly invested in new production technologies. (Photograph courtesy of Valmet)

somewhat derivative of a European design), they have proved themselves to be masters of the art of high technology mass-production systems. For Wiedeking to embrace the manufacturing philosophies of the Japanese would have been a difficult decision, but one that had to be taken if the company was to survive.

He took teams of people from the company to Japan where they worked day and night studying in minute detail exactly what took pace in each process along the production line. In addition, Wiedeking invited Japanese consultants to Stuttgart-Zuffenhausen to advise Porsche on the most efficient way to lay out the new production machinery.

It is possibly apocryphal, but reportedly one of the senior Japanese people charged with the responsibility of restructuring the production processes on a walk around the Zuffenhausen plant and seeing crates of components stacked to the ceiling, said to Wiedeking: 'Where's the factory? This is a warehouse!' Such was Porsche's dilemma.

So profound were the changes made by Wiedeking that the time taken to build a Porsche has been significantly reduced. For example, the last of the air-cooled 911s (the 993) took around 100 hours to build, while in comparison the new 996 takes half that time.

Previously Porsche made a considerable portion of the 911 and 928 in-house. The

New Production Technology

A Boxster body goes through the body dip to immerse it and deposit primer paint electrolytically throughout. (Photograph courtesy of Valmet)

Some painting processes at Porsche are still carried out by hand, such as applying the clear lacquer coat to a metallic colour.

Valmet has installed a robotized body spray-painting system that uses environmentally friendly water-based paints. (Photograph courtesy of Valmet)

A final inspection of the newly painted Boxster body is carried out before it is passed to the assembly area. (Photograph courtesy of Valmet)

After painting the body moves down the assembly line where the various components are added to its specification. With the complexity of today's cars, this is a long process. (Photograph courtesy of Valmet)

Large cradles hold the body at a convenient height for the assembly technician. Computers control the line's speed and coordinate the arrival of components from outside suppliers. (Photograph courtesy of Valmet)

New Production Technology

Opposite *The cradles holding the partly completed Boxster can be raised and lowered to suit the task at hand and the height of the workers. (Photograph courtesy of Valmet)*

Left *One of the more fascinating areas of the line is the mating of the mechanical components with the body. (Photograph courtesy of Valmet)*

924/944/968 family were different insofar as from the beginning they used components sourced from a variety of suppliers, components that were already in volume production for another manufacturer. This meant that at various places along the production path of the model through the factory were vast stores of components waiting for 'their' car to come by so they could be installed. Under the new regime, Porsche adopted the 'just-in-time' routine, whereby partner companies deliver their contracted components to Stuttgart-Zuffenhausen as and when they are required. In many instances, these supplier partners were also responsible for the engineering of their components to very strict Porsche standards.

Transmissions, for example, come from two sources: the VW Group (Audi AG) for the five- (and later) six-speed manual gearboxes; and long-standing supplier ZF of Friedrichshafen supplies the Tiptronic S five-speed automatic gearboxes. ThyssenKrupp Automotive manufacture the front and rear suspension sub-assemblies. However, Porsche alone retains responsibility for the design, development and production of its engines, something that it prides itself in doing well.

The Werke

The Porsche factory in Stuttgart-Zuffenhausen comprises three Werke. Werke 1 (the original works) on the Porschestrasse is today the company's headquarters and customer service centre.

Across the road is Werke 2, originally the premises of the carrozzeria Reutter. It is here that assembly of the engines takes place, where

New Production Technology

the bodies are painted and final assembly occurs. It is here where the new production system is on display as the engine–transmission–rear suspension assembly on its subframe is bolted to the body; the front suspension-steering subframe is likewise bolted up to the body; seats are installed as is the wiring loom, the dashboard and door trims. It is all a model of planned efficiency.

In Werke 3, the newest of Porsche's factories and built alongside Werke 1, is the body fabrication area where the many panels that go to make up a Boxster body are received (from BMW's factory in Eisenach), placed in jigs and robot-welded – there are more than seventy of them – to form the structure. They then cross the Porschestrasse through a 'glass bridge' to Werke 2 where they are cleaned, dipped and painted in a specially designed booth that uses water-based paints and meets all the tough anti-pollution laws.

Subcontracting to Valmet

Not only was Porsche AG involved in the production of the Boxster, but with demand from the dealers flooding into the factory the original production schedules that called for a rate of 12,000 units a year was going to be woefully inadequate. Management looked at a number of possibilities, from expanding Zuffenhausen to cooperation with another manufacturer. As it was not possible to expand the facilities at Zuffenhausen, it proved necessary in the short term to seek out a joint venture partner. But whom?

A small company in Finland, Valmet Automotive located in Uusikaupunki, was selected and a contract signed in the early months of 1997. Valmet had been founded in 1968 as an independent supplier of niche cars and a systems supplier of complete projects. The first car the company manufactured was the 1969 model Saab 96. Over 740,000 Saab 95, 96, 99, 900 and 9000 models have left the Valmet assembly line. And since 1986 some 198,000 Saab convertibles have been built.

In 1995 Valmet was awarded the ISO 9001 quality certification for the designing, engineering and manufacturing of passenger cars, a QS-9000 certificate was granted in 1999 and an ISO 14001 environmental certificate in 2001. From Porsche's point of view, Valmet was well qualified to meet the challenge of assembling the Boxster to standards that would meet the stringent requirements of Porsche.

The contract called for a production rate of 5,000 units a year. The first Boxster from Valmet rolled off the Uusikaupunki assembly line in September 1997. For Valmet this meant a 17 million investment in a new line designed to produce fifty vehicles in two shifts, but the process was quickly upgraded to produce one-hundred Boxsters a day. Meanwhile, the number of welding robots has increased from eight to more than thirty; continuing investment should eventually see sixty robots in use as more sub-assemblies are made at Valmet.

Such has been the pace of production that in August 2003 the one-hundred-thousandth Porsche Boxster was built. This has exceeded all expectations, with the annual rate of production from Uusikaupunki running at more than 20,000 units. In October 2001 Porsche AG and Valmet Automotive signed a continuity agreement on the contract to manufacture the Boxster that was valid until 2008 and had a further option until 2011.

Opposite *Before despatching each Boxster off to its international destination, a final check of all work is carried out.*

New Production Technology

12 Owning a Boxster Today

Owning a Porsche Boxster is the dream of many, many people. That is great, but there is nevertheless the caveat of which all prospective buyers should be abundantly aware. A Porsche Boxster is a man-made machine and it is not infallible. Sorry to shatter the myth!

A Boxster is, however, more bullet-proof than most cars and for a sports car that is likely to be driven hard and fast as often as possible on the road and on track drive days, it is amazingly reliable.

But there is no such thing as a bargain. As Nic Doczi from the Porsche Club Great Britain said, 'Normal rules of commerce apply no matter what price you paid. A good 1996–97 Boxster 2.5 will still cost around £18,000 and if major troubles occur parts and

Look into my eyes. A head-on view of a Porsche Boxster S on the Yorkshire moors in the late afternoon sun. (Gavin Farmer Library Collection)

Owning a Boxster Today

The Long and Winding Road

Edinburgh has always fascinated me, and so when the opportunity came from Porsche to drive the new Boxster S to the city from Surrey, I jumped at the chance.

Most people would suggest that a driving holiday to Scotland for a week or so in a sports car would require you taking leave of your senses. After all, conventional wisdom says that sports cars are uncomfortable and have no luggage room, that all your wife can take is her toothbrush and G-string! That may be the case with many conventional sports cars that are considered as rivals for the Boxster – the Mercedes-Benz SLK, for example, has a virtually unusable luggage compartment if you lower the clever folding roof, and the Z4 is limited to the one wide but shallow compartment – but it is definitely not with the Porsche Boxster.

Thoughtfully, Porsche designers and engineers have provided not one but two luggage carrying areas in the Boxster, a benefit of the car's mid-engined design. The basic essentials needed for a week away during the cool of autumn were packed into soft bags that fitted into the front compartment with relative ease. In the smaller compartment at the rear my wife and I were able to stow the camera gear, backpacks and other bits and pieces that you always take because you 'might' need them.

Our drive north from London on the infamous M1 via the equally infamous M25 began with few hassles as it was just after six-thirty in the morning and there were not many hardy souls out thrashing along the motorway at that early hour. The miles rolled by under the wide Michelin Pilot tyres as we cruised sedately at around 75mph, or 2,600rpm on the tachometer, in sixth gear. When the motorway presented the opportunity it was fun to slow and drop back to third gear and accelerate to the 7,200rpm red-line just to feel the sheer power and aural delights of the 260bhp Boxster S's flat-six engine as it pushed us very rapidly towards the horizon with consummate ease. The spacings between the gears were nigh-on perfect from third to fourth, then fifth and finally sixth gear. Each change kept the engine well within its power and torque band. And the gearshift was extremely accurate, if perhaps a little lacking in mechanical feel.

The miles disappeared with ease and soon we were in the Yorkshire Dales. By now the sun was out so we lowered the top to enjoy al fresco motoring across the Dales. Top down, the Boxster looked stunning, especially in a brilliant yellow that contrasted against the green of the Yorkshire countryside. The top folded down in 12sec at the press of a switch (once unlocked from the header rail, of course!). With the wind

The bright yellow Boxster in the grounds of Blackross Castle. (Gavin Farmer Library Collection)

The Long and Winding Road *continued*

blocker in place and the automatic air conditioning blowing warm air on to our legs – we set it at 24° – we were snug inside, and with the side windows up the buffeting from the wind was practically zero. And in this way we (well, me) could enjoy the aural delights of the flat-six engine as we raced across the Dales using the gears far more than necessary. When you do this you understand why it was so important in the development of the engine to get the exhaust tone just right – it is an essential and intrinsic part of the Porsche ownership experience.

Sadly, the sun disappeared and as we approached Scotland the rain started. It was cold outside – the dashboard gauge told us it was 7°C – but we were snug and warm inside the Boxster's cockpit. The wipers kept the screen clear, the heated element in the glass rear window kept that clear and the padded soft-top muffled the sound of the rain on the roof. And the Pirelli P6000 tyres kept us glued to the road.

The tactile steering with excellent weighting proved to be millimetre-accurate as we swept through bend after bend using second, third and fourth gears to the maximum. The aural delight of the flat-six engine rose and fell as the tachometer needle swung around the dial. Braking, too, was strong and consistent and even though there were puddles of water and potholes on many corners, the balance and very rapid progress of the Boxster S was unhindered. The tandem operation of the analogue speedometer matched to the digital read-out was fascinating

We arrived at Edinburgh at six o'clock in the evening. Our drive had taken twelve hours, but that had included a leisurely two-hour stopover in Bradford, once home to the Jowett motor car. Despite being in a powerful sports car, speed limits were in general adhered to, as I did not wish to jeopardize either my licence or my wallet by challenging the multitude of speed cameras encountered en route. The Porsche Boxster S proved to be a most capable and friendly travelling companion. Resplendent in its Speed Yellow livery with a black leather interior, it was noticed wherever we went. Its performance was staggering, as were its braking abilities and the ride-handling compromise was excellent for a sports car. Economy was good, too, although the comparatively small tank limited its range. The automatic air-conditioning system was easy to use and once set kept the interior cosy and warm and the windows mist-free. The BOSE sound system gave a quality of sound that would rival many home systems.

Sports car driving does not get much better than this. In fact, relatively affordable sports car driving is totally embodied in the Porsche Boxster S.

Boxster S resting by a rock formation, Yorkshire Dales. (Gavin Farmer Library Collection)

A beautiful sports car in a peaceful country setting. The Boxster is an ideal travelling companion.

labour will be as expensive as if you bought a far more expensive Boxster.'

The Boxster has been on the market for eight model years and has remained little changed in appearance, although there have been a myriad changes and upgrades as a normal part of the Porsche development programme.

Body

Porsche is one of a number of responsible manufacturers that offers buyers a ten-year warranty on the body. All body panels are fully galvanized steel and it is unlikely that a Boxster would be on offer with obvious rust. However, you need to be aware of the fact that the ten-year warranty only applies if the car has been inspected annually as part of the service programme at an Official Porsche Centre.

The most obvious potential problem to look for is signs of accident damage. It does not happen often, but some Boxsters that have been involved in an accident may have been taken to a non-Official Porsche Centre for repair. In many of those cases the alignment of body panels will not be what it ought to be – a sure sign to look elsewhere. In any case, it would be a good idea to put the car on a hoist and give the underbody and suspension pick-up points a thorough inspection.

Being a roadster, it is probable that a good percentage of the car's time will have been spent with the top down – that is, after all, why roadsters are purchased in the first place. This means that the interior will have been exposed directly to the elements, in particular the sun. This would not be quite the issue in somewhere like England as it would be for Boxsters sold in markets such as Australia, South Africa and the west coast of America.

Leather needs regular applications of condi-

Owning a Boxster Today

Owning a Boxster Today

Opposite *The Boxster's front view is typically Porsche. Some critics say it is too like the 911.*

Above *Possibly the best view of a Porsche Boxster – the three-quarter rear view.*

tioner – it's available as part of an overall car care package from your friendly local Porsche dealer – to keep it supple and prevent cracking. Feel the leather to see whether it is still supple or whether it has started to stiffen. Check also to see if the plastic finishes on the doors are still in good condition.

In any pre-2003 Boxster, look also for cracks in the plastic rear screen and even in the foldaway hood itself. A new plastic screen can be provided by an independent hood specialist, but, like the hood itself, is quite expensive.

There are one or two housekeeping items relating to the hood that new owners ought to be aware of. Firstly, if the weather is freezing cold – below 10°C or 50°F – do not lower the hood as the plastic rear screen will be cold and brittle, and will crack. Secondly, when cleaning the hood use only clean water – do not use a detergent, as the scouring effect of it will gradually ruin the waterproofing on the hood material. Thirdly, the rear window seems to collect fumes from the engine – clean the screen with warm water (no detergent again) and use a soft cloth to avoid scratching the surface.

When looking at a possible second-hand purchase, get the owner to lower the hood. This should be a totally smooth operation that takes between 12 and 14sec. If it takes longer, or the process of folding is jerky, the signs are that the hood has been damaged. Replacement folding hoods are very expensive, so either walk away or allow for the expense in the purchase offer.

And when lowering the top on pre-2003 model year Boxsters, there is a routine that you

Porsche has a great pedigree in motor racing, and the Boxster continues the proud tradition.

ought to follow. Lower the top halfway, get out of the car and gently push the screen in – it's called by Boxster owners giving the screen 'the chop!' This will ensure that the screen folds smoothly and without causing any damage. Obviously 'the chop' is not necessary on the 2003 onwards models as they have a glass screen – a major improvement.

Engine

Early 2.5-litre engines displayed signs of reliability problems with the occasional valve spring breaking, cracks appearing in the cylinder heads, the liners 'moving' and the rear main bearing oil seal weeping. Porsche was very quick to bring in manufacturing modifications to the point where the weeping of the rear main bearing oil seal is the only area of complaint from owners today. And do not form the impression that oil gushes out; it does not. The signs that it is going are small drops of oil on the driveway under the car. According to owners it is more of an annoyance than anything else. The later 2.7- and 3.2-litre engines have an excellent record.

If the oil and filter are not changed regularly it is possible for the VarioCam system to clog up and malfunction – it becomes a variocam (lower case intentional!) with no variance. The signs of this are poor running characteristics, poor idling and sometimes a stuttering when the throttle is opened. A thorough cleaning of the sensor, the Vario-Cam unit and a complete change of oil and filter usually fixes this problem – a problem caused not by a design fault but by poor maintenance.

With the development of the engine to 2.7- and 3.2 litres most of the early problem areas have been fixed.

Suspension

The early sports suspension option (mainly MY97) was hard and harsh to the point where dealers did not recommend to buyers that they tick the box on the order form. Porsche was made aware of this and for MY98 it was lowered less than previously.

Unless the Boxster has been driven into curbs and gutters the alignment of the front end retains its accuracy for long periods; and the service life of lower ball joints is measured in years.

The MacPherson strut suspensions front and rear have proven to be long-lived and largely trouble-free.

Brakes

The longevity of your brakes, in particular the front brakes, will depend on how hard you drive and how often you participate in Club track days. In general use, the rotors seem to last for around 25,000 miles (40,225km), or if the rotor has been worn by around 1.5mm. When the pads get down to 2mm the integral electrical contact will touch the rotor and a warning light will come on the dash advising the driver that the pads have reached the end of their safe working life.

There is a tendency for the drilled rotors on the Boxster S to get clogged with pad material and this can cause grooving of the discs, which means they will need to be replaced.

It is generally recommended that when the brake pads are renewed the rotors should also be replaced.

Battery

If there is a potential source of frustration, it is the battery. Do not leave your keys in the ignition for any long period of time as the entire electrical system will remain energized. If you do need to leave the key in the ignition shut the engine off, remove the key until you hear all the solenoids close and then reinsert the key. The electrical system will not re-energize again until you turn the key.

Also be aware that leaving items like the radar detector plugged into the cigarette lighter socket will drain the battery as that socket is live even with the ignition off.

If, for any reason, you do experience a flat battery call the Porsche Emergency Service and under the terms of the warranty it will arrange for your car to be returned to base on a truck and will fix the problem for you. If your car were out of warranty there would be a charge for this service.

13 Old Versus New: The 914 vs 986

Comparisons, some people say, are odious and unnecessary. Well, they are entitled to their opinion, but in real life no matter what field of endeavour we are engaged in we are constantly comparing this with that. Product or service, it matters not. And cars are not immune from comparisons – quite the reverse in fact!

From the beginning, Porsche wanted to draw a parallel between the 550 Spyder and the Boxster, that one inspired the other. From the purely aesthetic point of view there can be little or no argument about this fact, although many Porsche experts contend that the more realistic inspiration was in fact the 'Butzi' Porsche designed RS61 Spyder. However, there is another long-forgotten Porsche, one that Porsche true believers wish had never happened. It did, and it was a big contributor to the company's coffers at the time and proudly carried the famous antlered crest. So let's not hide away from the past and let us look at the Boxster in relation to its far older stepbrother, the 914.

The similarities between the 914 and the 986 are amazing, given the passing of around twenty years from the end of one model's lifespan and the beginning of the other's. They differ in their origins – the 914 was a sports car of mixed parentage, while the 986 Boxster was

The 914 was quite a controversial sports car in 1970, but the driving experience of the 914/6 more than made up for that.

A quarter of a century apart in concept and style, but nevertheless similarities are evident. (Photograph courtesy of D. Fagan)

a pure-bred Porsche – but the 914 was the world's first mass-produced mid-engined sports car, a mantle that the Boxster took up with some vigour.

The similarities between the two cars are evident in the longitudinally positioned mid-located engine with five-speed transaxle, fully independent suspension system, two-seater configuration (although the 914 was actually designed to be a three-seater, the third person having to sit on a small flat ledge between the two actual seats, this being the reason why the handbrake lever is by the driver's door sill) and luggage compartments at both ends of the vehicles. There would be those who would suggest that the 914 was the template for the 986. Would they be wrong or just one-eyed?

From the first press reports in 1969 the styling of the 914 attracted considerable comment. *Sports Car Graphic* from America headlined its opening article with the words 'It'll Grow on You'. *Road Test* magazine's contributor wrote, 'After viewing the sleek lines of the 911, the slab-sided 914 requires a little visual adjustment. The abundance of sharp corners on wings and roof line in side and end views is very un-Porsche like.' Jonathan Thompson, writing in *Road & Track*, commented:

> I do not find the front-end styling attractive. Retractable headlights are In, of course. They usually make a nose look sleeker when down and spoil the lines when up; this is true of the 914. The 914 also has pinched-looking front fenders and an insensitively designed front bumper, a fairly massive piece of black rubber for the size of the car.

As we know, the Boxster suffered much the same criticism from those who had seen the concept car and admired its proportions but ignored the fact that as it was displayed it would not meet critically important safety and packaging requirements.

Old Versus New: The 914 vs 986

The business end of each: the Boxster is the more rounded, softer shape and is superior aerodynamically. (Photograph courtesy of D. Fagan)

Both sports roadsters featured low and functional styling – note the similarity of angle of the lights and windscreen rake. (Photograph courtesy of D. Fagan)

From a purely physical-dimensions point of view the two Porsches were remarkably close: the 914's wheelbase was 96.5in (2,450mm) compared with the Boxster's 95.2in (2,418mm), while the greater overall length of the Boxster – 171in versus 157in (4,343mm v 3,912mm) – was attributable to the longer front and rear overhangs necessary to meet the aforementioned safety requirements. The Boxster was wider by 5in (127mm) and heavier by a staggering 700lb (316kg), again mostly attributable to the needs of protecting the car's occupants in a collision. This was never a consideration at the time of the signing-off of the 914's design and engineering.

Taken from the 911 Targa was the same rollover protection for 914 owners, a feature not present in the Boxster, although there are stout rollover hoops behind both seats for the very same reason.

In their architecture, the two mid-engined Porsches are identical, with luggage compartments front and rear. And like the 986, the 914 made use of much of the frontal structure of the then current 911 as well as the space-saving longitudinally located torsion bar front suspension system. At the rear, of course, the 914 had its own unique semi-trailing arm with a coil-over-damper suspension because the disposition of the engine and transmission precluded the use of the 911 torsion bar system.

The more expensive 914/6 used a 911 T 125bhp 2.0-litre version of the company's famous air-cooled flat six. In this guise the 914's performance was considered to be very quick by the standards of 1969/70, with a maximum speed of around 125mph (200km/h) and a 0–60mph time of 8.5sec. The more powerful and bigger capacity engined Boxster has been timed in the 0–60mph sprint at 6.7sec by most publications, a less than 2sec advantage for more than twenty years of technological improvement. Top speed was generally quoted as 140mph (225km/h), again superior because of the greater engine capacity and power plus vastly better aerodynamics, a crucial factor in the higher speed registers.

The most obvious divergence in engine technology was the late adoption of water-cooling by Porsche after building its tradition around the simplicity and reliability – and the sheer logic – of air-cooling. Along with Tatra, Porsche was the last to make the change to water-cooling and in many respects it was done purely to satisfy the ever-growing raft of bureaucratic regulations rather than for any engineering reason. In this respect, the 914 was a child of rather more innocent times.

What both Porsches did was to raise the bar of expectation with respect to roadholding and handling. We have already read how today's Boxster is the best sports car package in terms of roadholding and handling, even seven years after its release and the arrival of new-generation rivals. The 914, too, was considered the best of its genre thirty years ago. What was the 914 competing against? In 1970 Nissan released the epochal Datsun 240Z, the car that virtually single-handedly brought the British sports car industry to its knees simply because the British refused to invest in new ideas – they kept plugging away at the international markets with the MGB and TR6, both of which were characterful but old and in dire need of re-engineering into something more in keeping with the times. As we know, that never happened, because you could not in all honesty include the lamentable TR7 as a 'sports' car. The main British contender against the 914 was the Triumph TR6 and from Italy came the Fiat 124 Spider. With the notable exception of the 914, all were traditional front engine/rear wheel drive cars and only the 240Z, like the 914, had a fully independent suspension system.

From a sports car point of view, the 0–60mph sprint is crucial and here the 914/4 was the slowest – 13.9sec versus 11.9 for the Fiat, 10.7 for the Triumph and 8.7sec for the 240Z according to a *Road & Track* comparison. The 914/6, a far more expensive machine, took just 8.5sec.

The Autocar from England, which was to carry out many 914 tests, compared the Porsche with several rivals and published the data given in the table at the foot of the page. The same magazine wrote glowingly of the 914's dynamics:

> On corners the 914 is a revelation, staying flat on the road and true to line whatever the speed. One no longer thinks in terms of front and rear ends separately because the car is such an integrated unit, seeming to do everything from its centre, where all the weight is concentrated. On the road handling reserves are tremendous and matched

	Porsche 914/4	**Datsun 240Z**	**Fiat 124 Spider**	**Triumph TR6**
List price (USD)	$3,695	$3,526	$3,450	$3,425
Kerb weight, lb	2,085	2,355	2,090	2,360
0–60mph, sec	13.9	8.7	11.9	10.7
Standing ¼ mile	19.2	17.1	18.3	17.9
Speed at end, mph	70	84.5	76	77
Economy, mpg	25.5	21.0	24.5	20.7

Old Versus New: The 914 vs 986

	Porsche 914/4	Lotus Europa S2	TVR Vixen S2	MGB GT	Matra M530A
Max speed	102mph	110+mph	109mph	101mph	95mph
0–60mph, sec	14.8	9.4	10.5	13.6	15.6
Standing ¼ mile, sec	19.9	16.9	17.2	19.1	19.9
Economy, mpg	20.5	23.1	26.5	22.8	26.9

This is the later and vastly improved 2-litre 914 with US bumpers and factory alloy wheels. One of the endearing features of the 914 was the removable Targa roof that could be stored in the rear luggage compartment.

only in our experience by four-wheel drive. Quick directional reversals, like winding lanes, roundabouts and natural chicanes bring the 914 right out into its element in a way that no sports car (short of a Lotus) has ever done before.

Jerry Sloniger, writing for the Australian publication *Sports Car World*, said after a test drive session of a 914/6 at Hockenheim,

> This six has the same sort of balance (as a 908 racer); same wrist-flick control and fun quotient simply reduced to terms we average drivers can master.
>
> With only 2 turns of the wheel you can wish a 914 around bends, catch the tail with a nudge of the hands or pitch it sideways and laugh. Weight balance of 45/55 does no harm. Adhesion is so good first corners are taken far below the limits in sheer disbelief.

Similar eulogies were written about the 914/6, always with the proviso of price. Again *Road & Track* published a chart to explain the major comparative points with its rivals.

Both *Road & Track* and *The Autocar* were full of praise for the handling characteristics of the 914/6, citing the wider rims and tyres as the main contributors and offering the thought that the 914 chassis could easily cope with considerably more power than the 125bhp offered by the current model.

By the 1972 model year the rather expensive 911-powered 914/6 was dropped from the model range and replaced by the 914 SC. Still of 2-litre capacity, it was a Porsche-devel-

	Porsche 914/6	**Lotus Elan S4 SE**	**Alfa Romeo 1750 Spider**	**Jaguar E-Type**
List price (USD)	$6,099	$5,133	$4,333	$5,675
Kerb weight, lb	2,195	1,630	2,346	3,018
0–60mph, sec	8.7	9.4	9.9	8.0
Standing ¼ mile	16.3	16.8	17.3	15.7
Speed at end, mph	83	83	80	86
Economy, mpg	21.3	27.2	21.5	15.9

oped version of the VW 411 air-cooled four-cylinder engine.

Media reports were favourable by and large as Porsche played with the equipment lists and made more items a standard fitting where previously they were optional and did not raise the price significantly compared with the outgoing 914. As *Road & Track* wrote: 'The price will keep the 914/2 from being a sports car for the masses but with the extra torque, the improved gearshift, the handling and the extra quality of the exhaust note, the 914/2 is one of the better sports cars around.'

While Porsche has never sanctioned rallying or racing the Boxster, it did homologate the 914 in Groups 4 and 6 and contested the gruelling 24 Hours of Le Mans with some success. And the factory built two wild 914 prototypes powered by the competition 908 engine. One was owned and driven for many years by none

Porsche tried to create an image of the 914 benefiting one's lifestyle in much the same way as it does today. Owning your own light plane and a Porsche 914 made perfect sense. The 914 is one of the very few German cars to have featured pop-up headlights.

Old Versus New: The 914 vs 986

A real wolf in sheep's clothing – one of just two 914's built powered by the 908 racing boxer air-cooled engine. Ferdinand Piëch owned and drove one for many years.

other than Ferdinand Piëch. Both 908-powered 914s still exist.

Like many die-hard Porsche 914 enthusiasts, leading English authority on the model, David Fagan (who incidentally owns a 914/6 and a Boxster), looks upon the current Boxster as a 914/6 'evo', the lower case being intentional.

While all 914s built by Porsche – actually Karmann in Osnabrück built the bodies under contract – were left-hand drive, the English company Crayford did convert between ten and twelve 914s to right-hand drive, but the cost of the conversion, when added to the purchase price of the car, meant that the total price was almost the same as for a 911.

Many so-called expert commentators on Porsche have described the 914 as the company's greatest folly, and while it may not have been as successful in Europe as Porsche (and VW) had hoped, it was very successful in America. As the American Porsche expert Joe Rusz wrote in his book *Porsche Sport 1976/77*, 'the 914's life was short but prolific. It was the most popular Porsche ever sold – 83,841 units (US) in seven years. And it was controversial – a Porsche to some, a Volkswagen to others.'

	Porsche 914	Porsche 914/2	Porsche 914/6	Datsun 240Z	Jensen-Healey	Lotus Europa
Max speed	109mph	119mph	123mph	125mph	120mph	121mph
0–60mph	13.9sec	10.3sec	8.7sec			
0–50mph				8.3sec	7.5sec	6.6sec
Standing ¼ mile	19.2sec	17.8 sec	16.3 sec			16.9sec
Economy	25.5mpg	24.5mpg	21.3mpg	26mpg	21mpg	24mpg

Old Versus New: The 914 vs 986

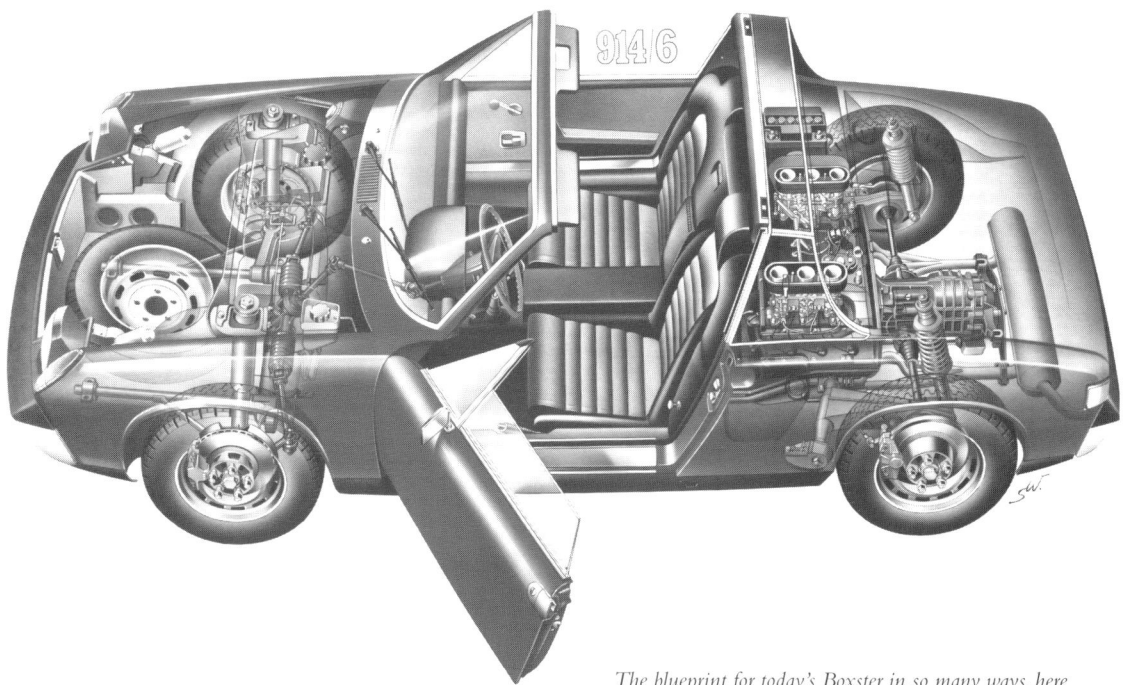

The blueprint for today's Boxster in so many ways, here exposed in all its technical glory: 911 torsion bar front suspension and steering, semi-trailing arm coil spring IRS, four-wheel disc brakes and the fabulous flat-six engine.

If the growl of the racing engine did not give the game away, a peak at the tachometer red-lined at 9,000rpm would!

Appendix I
VIN Coding for Boxsters

First Eleven Characters	Model Year	Build Location
WP0ZZZ98ZVS	1997	Stuttgart
WP0ZZZ98ZWS	1998	Stuttgart
WP0ZZZ98ZWU	1998	Uusikaupunki
WP0ZZZ98ZXS	1999	Stuttgart
WP0ZZZ98ZXU	1999	Uusikaupunki
WP0ZZZ98ZYS	2000	Stuttgart
WP0ZZZ98ZYU	2000	Uusikaupunki
WP0ZZZ98Z1S	2001	Stuttgart
WP0ZZZ98Z1U	2001	Uusikaupunki
WP0ZZZ98Z2S	2002	Stuttgart
WP0ZZZ98Z2U	2002	Uusikaupunki
WP0ZZZ98Z3S	2003	Stuttgart
WP0ZZZ98Z3U	2003	Uusikaupunki
WP0ZZZ98Z4S	2004	Stuttgart
WP0ZZZ98Z4U	2004	Uusikaupunki

The VIN number is located in the right-hand doorjamb.

Information supplied by Porsche Club Great Britain.

Appendix II
Model Year Differences

To the untrained eye all Porsche Boxsters appear to be the same because their styling has remained basically untouched from the beginning. But how appearances deceive! There have been a myriad small changes, some significant as part of the on-going evolution of the model (for which Porsche is famous) and others that are cosmetic.

MY97
This was the original model year for the start of Boxster production. Two options were available for buyers:

Luxury Pack at £4,515

Leather seats
Air-conditioning
Wind deflector
17in wheels and tyres
On-board computer

Sports Pack at £3,600

Leather upholstery
Traction control
Wind deflector
17in wheels and tyres
Firmer and lower (10mm) springs and dampers

MY98
18in wheels became available as a factory option. Along with this option came a significant improvement in the rigidity of the rear structure of the body as a result of field experience gained from tuners in Germany in particular. For MY98 the following areas were reinforced:

- rear wall cross member
- engine compartment bulkhead
- wheel well spring strut mount
- rear axle mount.

MY99
The fuel tank was increased in capacity from 57 to 64 litres by installing the 996 tank. Storage space was improved: a small drawer below the steering column for the driver's manual or road maps (Note: not *and* road maps!).

Litronic headlights were available as an option.

There was automatic door locking that could be programmed in four ways by the dealer:

1. Doors lock automatically when the ignition is turned on.
2. Doors lock automatically when the car's speed exceeds 4mph.
3. Doors lock automatically when the ignition is switched on; if the doors are opened with the engine running, they will lock automatically again when the car's speed exceeds 4mph.
4. Doors do not lock automatically – this was the factory default.

Note: When the doors are locked automatically

a red LED illuminates in the central locking button. Automatically locked doors can be opened with the central locking button or by pulling on the inside door handle twice.

MY00
Porsche owners (and the media) said that the 2.5-litre engine was not powerful enough. The factory's response was two-fold – two engines were now on the menu, a 2.7-litre version for the 'basic' Boxster and a powerhouse 3.2-litre version for the Boxster S.

Compared to the Boxster 2.7, the Boxster S had:

- 3.2-litre engine with upgraded Motronic DME unit
- six-speed manual gearbox
- firmer springs, stabilizer bars and dampers
- longer rear axle control arms for toe-in angle retention
- larger wheel bearings for camber angle retention
- 996 brakes: larger diameter rotors, cross-drilled, larger red painted calipers
- higher torque capacity Tiptronic S gearbox
- 17in wheels standard
- three-spoke steering wheel standard
- remote alarm system standard
- variable intermittent wipers
- centre front air intake in the bumper
- centre front fluid radiator
- soft-top roof liner
- vanity mirror light
- bright aluminium instrument bezels and silver-faced instruments
- 170mph analogue speedometer
- sill panels with 'Boxster S' logo
- Titanium trim colour: exterior windscreen frame, radiator grilles (not the centre one), 'S' on the boot lid
- dual exhaust pipes
- relocated cruise control indicator
- more weight by 77lb

- added coefficient of drag (Cd), taking it to 0.32
- less economy by approximately 2mpg
- POSIP airbag protection system.

MY01
Changes began to accelerate with MY01 as the competition became more intense:

- new cloth lining in the folding hood for both Boxsters
- integrated safety bars now covered with a soft-touch material
- new three-spoke steering wheel with coloured Porsche crest
- both models had LED interior lights that provided gentle illumination of the cockpit, console, ignition lock and door latches
- the trunk release levers were changed from cable pulls to electric switches
- improved carpeting in the trunks; carpet colour changed from grey to black
- the spoiler light stayed on longer after you started the car; different dash light to show that one or both trunks were open
- the electric windows had an auto-retract system if they sensed an obstruction
- when raising the top, the side windows went back up when the top latch had been closed
- new fuel cap design: no longer hung on the fuel filler door but was attached by a rubberized strap so it could not be inadvertently lost
- improved sound system
- Porsche Stability Management (PSM) available on both models.

MY02
Again, plenty of detail change to keep the market interested:

- the seat belts now incorporated pretensioners and force limiters
- a new multi-function display unit in the instrument cluster when the optional on-board computer (OBC) was ordered

- keys now had a coloured Porsche crest
- dashboard switches now had a matte finish (previously gloss)
- cup holder in the centre of the dash
- anti-entrapment trunk release with internal handle
- new colours: Black, Carrera White, Black Basalt Metallic
- new BOSE® sound system that replaced the previous digital sound system.

MY03
Further refinements made the MY03 Boxsters by far the best yet:

- increased horsepower due to the new Vario-Cam Plus system: +8bhp both models
- S only: marginally improved torque: +3lb ft
- nominally better fuel mileage: +2 per cent for both models
- new front and rear bumpers with a prominent ridge on the lower edge
- clear indicator lenses front and rear, also side repeaters
- side air intakes reshaped, integrated surround and grilles, now body colour
- redesigned spoiler, also slightly larger
- glass rear window
- lockable glovebox with light
- 996 centre console
- horizontal switches
- cup holders under the centre air vent; air vents slightly smaller
- no sports or sports touring packages
- CDR-23 in-dash CD player standard uses MOST® fibre-optic bus
- Midnight Blue added to colour selection
- 18in wheels from the Carrera
- standard and optional wheels were all lighter
- Porsche Communication Management (PCM) II optional.

Appendix III
Suspension Setting for Track Days

Front

	Standard Tolerances	Track day settings (Sport)
Toe-in	+5' +/− 5'	0.00'
Camber	−10' +/−30'	Maximum negative achievable

Rear

	Standard Tolerances	Track day settings (Sport)
Toe-in	+5' +/−5'	−0° 05'
Camber	−1° 20' +/−30'	Maximum negative Achievable up to −2°

NOTE: If you have a Sports suspension you can achieve greater negative camber but you will need to take care to avoid uneven or excessive tyre wear.

Tyre Pressures
Boxsters do not require much differential between front and rear tyres. For track days the suggestion is to run with 32psi at the front and 34psi at the rear initially (these pressures are also very good for road use), checking the tyre pressures after each run to reach 38/40 when hot. The outside tyres will heat up more during track driving as they take more of the load; try to keep the pressures even across the axle; look for even temperatures across the tread and tread rollover. If there are signs of tread rollover, increase the tyre pressures.

- Make sure you adjust the pressures before you drive home.

- The ideal tyre pressure will vary from one brand of tyre to another.

Information from Nic Doczi, Porsche Club Great Britain.

Appendix IV
Customizing Your Boxster

Exclusive Line
There are two ways to customize your Porsche Boxster: the Exclusive Programme and Tequipment. The critical difference between the two is when the equipment is added to the car. With the Exclusive Programme the additional items are added to the Boxster as it moves along the assembly line – in other words, the car is built to the special order of a particular client who has ordered the car through an authorized Porsche dealer. Porsche proudly boasts that within reason anything is possible when it comes to ordering exclusive pieces of equipment to one of their cars.

Tequipment for the Boxster
Many owners who like to personalize their Boxster and Porsche have developed a range of extras that can enhance the ownership experience. All Porsche equipment is covered by the terms of the factory warranty and has been specifically designed by Porsche to be both elegant and functional.

A popular fitting is the Aerokit II that has been designed to minimize front and rear aerodynamic lift at high speeds. The offering for the Boxster was developed from the kit originally designed for the current 911 GT3. The stylish front spoiler is combined with a special rear wing with an integrated high intensity LED brake light and matching side skirts. It does make the Boxster and Boxster S look more masculine and purposeful. A point to be aware of here: Porsche will not provide you with just the front or just the rear spoiler; you must buy the complete package for reasons of safety.

In addition to the standard production alloy wheels Porsche offers a wide range of optional wheel styles that are designed to reduce the unsprung weight to increase the responsiveness of the Boxster's on-road (or track) performance. For the 2003 model year the company had nine wheel styles available, including in the 18in range the SportTechno, SportDesign, SportClassic II, Carrera and Turbo Look II and several 17in designs for tyres from either Pirelli or Continental.

If you wish, you can fit a set of wheel spacers or you can set off each wheel with a wheel centre that comes with the Porsche Crest; or you might want to cap the valve with a sleeve that is embossed with the Crest. A set of anti-theft wheel bolts would also be recommended.

A sports suspension kit that includes a full set of springs, dampers and anti-roll bars is designed to enhance the cornering power of your Boxster. The ride height is 10mm lower and it is slightly firmer than standard.

On the inside, owners can choose from an aluminium look, dark burr walnut or carbon interior to go with an in-car system that includes navigation, mobile communication and a selection of superior audio systems. All are linked by the MOST® bus technology that uses fibre-optics for high-speed data transfer. Boxsters built prior to July 2002 are linked by PCM (version 1) that uses digital technology.

Automatically dimming interior and exterior rear view mirrors are ideal for reducing glare from following cars. An optoelectronic sensor monitors the intensity of the headlights from following vehicles and dims the mirrors automatically.

For the ultimate in headlight performance Porsche offers the Litronic kit, which features Xenon technology for a whiter and brighter light that is free of glare to on-coming drivers.

If you enjoy touring and you need to carry more luggage than will fit into the front and rear compartments there are several alternatives. For example, there is the roof transport system; a rear mounted rack system; a bike carrier as well as the obligatory ski/snowboard carrier.

And if you do not have a garage to shelter your Boxster from the elements, Porsche offers a fabric cover that is breathable, anti-static and has the Crest emblazoned on it.

Appendix V
Production

Model Year	Location	Total	
1996/1997	Stuttgart	15,902	
1997/1998	Stuttgart	10,935	
	Uusikaupunki	7,952	Yr: 18,887
1998/1999	Stuttgart	8,608	
	Uusikaupunki	13,455	Yr: 22,063
1999/2000	Stuttgart	9,062	
	Uusikaupunki	16,803	Yr: 25,865
2000/2001	Stuttgart	5,163	
	Uusikaupunki	23,294	Yr: 28,457
2001/2002	Stuttgart	1,652	
	Uusikaupunki	20,337	Yr: 21,989
2002/2003	Stuttgart	757	
	Uusikaupunki	18,031	Yr: 18,788

Source: Porsche AG.

Appendix VI
Comparison Charts

Porsche Model Comparison – Non-Rear-Engined

	914 1.7	914 2.0 6-cyl	914 2.0 4-cyl	Boxster 2.5	Boxster 2.7	Boxster 3.2S
Engine						
Type	4-cyl, ohv, air-cooled, boxer	6-cyl, sohc, air-cooled, boxer	4-cyl, ohv, air-cooled, boxer	6-cyl, dohc water-cooled, boxer	<<	<<
Bore x stroke	90 x 66mm	80 x 66mm	94 x 71mm	85.5 x 72mm	85 x 78mm	93 x 78mm
Capacity	1,679cc	1,991cc	1,971cc	2,480cc	2,687cc	3,179cc
Comp	8.2:1	8.6:1	8.0:1	11.0:1	<<	<<
Intake	EFI	2 x Weber	EFI	DME 5.2	DME 7.2	<<
Power	85/4,900	125/5,800	100/5,000	204/6,000	220/6,400	252/6,250
Torque	103/2,800	131/4,200	115/3,500	181/4,500	192/4,750	225/4,500
Trans						
Type	5-sp man/ Sportomatic	5-sp man/ <<	5-sp man	5-sp man/ 5-sp auto	<<	6-sp man/ 5-sp auto
Axle ratio	4.43:1	4.43:1	4.43:1	3.88:1	3.88:1	3.44:1
Brakes						
Type	Disc/disc	<<	<<	4 disc, ABS	<<	<<
Perf						
0–100km/h	13.9sec	8.7sec	9.1sec	6.5sec	6.4sec	5.7sec
Max speed	109mph	123mph	115mph	139mph	149mph	161mph
1st	28mph	33mph	30mph	35mph	38mph	42mph
2nd	48mph	57mph	50mph	59mph	62mph	71mph
3rd	72mph	82mph	73mph	89mph	93mph	102mph
4th	97mph	105mph	100mph	122mph	129mph	127mph
5th						153mph
Economy	25.5mpg	21.3mpg	23.3mpg	27mpg	25.1mpg	21.4mpg
Weight	2,085lb	2,195lb	2,145lb	2,732lb	2,750kg	2,850kg
Prod						
Dates	9/69–7/93	9/69–6/72	8/72–12/75	10/96–7/99	8/99–7/02	8/99–7/02
Number built	115,597	3,338	121,510	55,705	75,509	<<